Ahrends Burton and Koralek

ARCHITECTURAL
Monographs

Ahrends Burton and Koralek

Introduction by Peter Blundell-Jones

ACADEMY EDITIONS · LONDON   ST. MARTIN'S PRESS · NEW YORK

With gratitude to all who taught us about architecture

Publisher
Dr Andreas C Papadakis

Published in Great Britain in 1991 by
ACADEMY EDITIONS
An imprint of the Academy Group Ltd, 7 Holland St
London W8 4NA

Subscriptions and Editorial Offices
7 Holland Street, London W8

HB 0 85670 929 8
PB 0 85670 927 1

Published in the United States of America in 1991
by
ST. MARTIN'S PRESS
175 Fifth Avenue, New York, NY 10010

HB 0-312-06191-9
PB 0-312-06192-7

Printed and bound in Singapore

Contents

Ahrends Burton and Koralek
an Introduction
Peter Blundell-Jones

When the history of architecture in late 20th Century Britain comes to be written, ABK will have to be given a major place in the three decades between 1960 and 1990, because of the sheer range and quality of their work and their central role in the British scene. Even so, their oeuvre may prove difficult to categorise, for it boasts neither the consistency associated with the signature of a single dominant designer, nor that resulting from the dogged pursuit of a constant theoretical viewpoint. Instead, the work varies enormously in its aims and character, and it is almost impossible to deduce the separate contributions of the three founder partners. All three are active designers and they take on major projects in turn. The office ethos is an imaginative response to the task in hand, including a general openness to new constructional and technical possibilities, a decidedly empirical approach.

Peter Ahrends, Richard Burton and Paul Koralek were all born in 1933 and first met as students at the Architectural Association in 1951, working together on group projects from early on. This was the period of the Festival of Britain, which symbolised the end of wartime rationing and austerity, the beginning of a new and better world. Architecturally, it marked a general acceptance of Modernism, for though the new style had gained a toe-hold in the thirties, it now became the vehicle for the architecture of the welfare state, typified by the Hertfordshire schools programme. For the three students the festival was an especially memorable event. Burton's stepfather, Gerald Barry, was involved in the preparations, so he at least saw behind the scenes and met most of the architects involved. They attribute their later interest in social building types – such as schools, libraries and hospitals – to attitudes imbibed and developed at this time.

The AA in the fifties was also a breeding ground for what was later called New Brutalism, an architecture in which virtue was made of expressed construction. The initial impetus came from Le Corbusier, who started to use board-marked concrete in a sculptural way in post-war works such as the Unité at Marseilles; quite the opposite of the smooth white atectonic surfaces of his early villas. The Unité was imitated fairly directly in a large housing development at Roehampton in south west London, designed by four LCC architects who set up a practice together in in 1959: William Howell, John Killick, John Partridge and Stanley Amis. They went on to explore the architectural implications of contrasting textures and materials, always self-consciously detailed; frame and infill, in-situ with pre-cast concrete.

That the Miesian model could also be given a Brutalist interpretation was demonstrated by Alison and Peter Smithson with their competition winning Hunsstanton school of 1949, completed in 1954. This was achieved not only by exploitation of the steel frame detailing contrasting with the original infill, but also by putting all the services – notably the plumbing – on display. Both John Killick of HPKA and Peter Smithson taught at the AA in the fifties, and their buildings were widely known. It is therefore not surprising to find a strong Brutalist flavour in the early work of ABK and a continuing interest in the poetics of construction. Unlike HPKA, this is not the focus of their interest in building, however, but rather a constituent part of their architectural sensibility.

The widespread interest in Le Corbusier and Mies van der Rohe running through British architecture generally, and the AA more particularly, during the fifties could scarcely be avoided. However, ABK were much more taken with the unfashionable Frank Lloyd Wright and his mentor Louis Sullivan, which earned them the nickname 'the country boys'. This was perhaps a significant choice, as Bruno Zevi had attempted to build his history of an alternative Modernist tradition, *Towards an Organic Architecture*, around the figure of Wright a few years earlier. ABK's interest in space and light as opposed to form, in process as much as product, in architecture as the unpredicted outcome of specific conditions, rather than as the imposition of a preconceived notion, all point towards the Wrightian vision of 'the thing growing out of the nature of the thing' as opposed to the universalist stance of the orthodox Modernist.

It was Louis Sullivan who coined the phrase 'Form follows function', while Wright reinterpreted his master's slogan as 'Form and function are one'. Although 'Functionalism' has become thoroughly unfashionable, it remains a touchstone for ABK, not interpreted narrowly or mechanistically as all too often in the early post-war years, but in the sense that use remains the starting point for design. With hindsight, one can see that for both American masters, it was the rhetoric of use rather than use itself that was important. 'The promise of function' as the sculptor Horation Greenough put it. For ABK too, the continuing fascination of the functionalist ethic is bound up with the question of how use gives rise to meaning.

A second aspect of Wright's work that has proved extremely influential is his use of geometric grids and controlling systems, which run through his work consistently from site-plan down to ornamental detail, employed both pragmatically and ideologically. The grid-planning in ABK's work is generally of a Wrightian open-ended kind rather than the more mechanistic variety normally met in Britain. Their interest in geometry was also sharpened by a visit to Turkey and Iran in 1956, where they became fascinated by the interlocking patterns and geometries of Islamic architecture contextually seen in relation to the structure of cities, towns and villages.

By the time they left the AA in 1956, Ahrends Burton and Koralek had decided to set up partnership together as soon as they could gain a commission, working meanwhile in the offices of others. Ahrends went back to his native South Africa for two years to work for his father Steffen before returning to join the London office of Denys Lasdun. Burton worked for the LCC for a year before joining Powell and Moya. Koralek also spent a year with Powell and Moya before working visits to France and Canada and ended up with Marcel Breuer in New York.

Ahrends and Burton completed a few small jobs in the name of the nascent practice while Koralek was working abroad, and it was partly because he felt guilty about not pulling his weight that the latter decided to enter the competition for Trinity Library, Dublin. He won first prize and the commission in 1961, which provided the long awaited opportunity to set up an office, and the design was developed by the partners together. This proved a heaven-sent opportunity for the three young architects, who were not yet thirty at the time, and it probably received more concentrated attention than any subsequent work, remaining a milestone both for the practice and for British architecture.

The competition jury seems to have no doubts about the choice of winner, and comparison with the other published competition entries twenty-eight years later vindicates their choice, for the clarity of conception in Koralek's scheme is still striking while it also seems visually less dated than its fellows. The master-stroke was the creation of a raised podium in front of the building containing a basement bookstore. This reduced the bulk of the library and gave it a base to sit on, but more importantly it made a virtue of a difficult site. To avoid crowding its neighbours – two Neo-Classical set pieces – the library had to be set back from New Square, creating a forecourt between them continuous with the square. Raising this forecourt with steps on its front edge gave it enough separate identity to read as an outdoor room on its own account rather than as a leaky corner of the main square. As a positive space, a cour d'honneur, it became an extension of the elaborate spatial progression within the new library, while also forging the required connection with the existing library on the right; the attempts by other competitors to achieve this by means of glazed links seem clumsy in comparison.

A less obvious merit of the design is the way it refused to be cramped or dulled by a completely regular and repetitive structure. The box-like upper floors containing the reading rooms were relieved in the competition design by a ground floor of asymmetrical layout and irregular perimeter, winding in and out of the columns, and in the built version the eruption of local incidents on the perimeter is extended to the first floor, only the second asserting the severity of the whole. These games of plan-libre against the discipline of the column system, are of course not arbitrary, but a means of accommodating within and expressing without, the local idiosyncrasies of the functional programme. It is this kind of detail which produces an external form of such liveliness and variety without violating the wholeness of the building.

Readers approaching the building from New Square ascend the steps to cross the forecourt, approaching the building directly but asymmetrically; the doors on axis with the steps. They cross a kind of porch created by the projection of the building above then enter a foyer space from which they can proceed directly to the catalogue room beyond, or up stairs or lift to the reading rooms above. The stairs are placed asymmetrically in the length of the building to create a major and minor end. The major one – the main reading room – is celebrated by a square well linking the two upper floors, the necessary focus of the library. In the built version the well is smaller, presumably for economic reasons, but it is made more powerful by the omission of the columns which interrupted the competition version. The final version also has a series of dramatic north-orientated rooflights, the highest occuring appropriately over the well, as opposed to the more regular skylights envisaged in the competition version.

Trinity Library still seems an outstanding building for its time, and an impressive accomplishment for such a young firm. It was more unusual than it seems now because of the attention given to the forecourt and siting; in the early sixties buildings were more generally conceived as free-standing objects. But for all its exceptional qualities, there is nothing revolutionary about its architectural language, for it merely combines – in new ways admittedly – the known elements of an existing Modernist vocabulary. ABK's work has continued in this vein, always thoughful, well considered, picking up on a rich variety of sources while remaining within the current tradition. This reflects the essential empiricism of their approach.

Trinity Library gave the young practice a good start, and they soon gained many further commissions for educational and cultural buildings. With public libraries in Maidenhead and Redcar, and the Polytechnic Library in Portsmouth, they demonstrated that repetition of a building type need not result in a repetitive architecture. Each of these buildings has a different character according to its programme and circumstances, and they do not share the same vocabulary of materials.

ABK also received commissions for a number of university and college buildings of which the best known are Chichester Theological College and the extension to Keble Oxford. Also at Oxford is their delightful Roman Catholic Chaplaincy which extends the Old Palace, a gabled seventeenth century timber-frame building in the heart of the city. It is a proud modern building without attempting to hide the fact, yet retains the scale of its neighbour and makes the most of its corner entrance; remarkably contextual for the uncontextual late sixties. In the conservationist eighties, no doubt many a planning committee would frown at its large areas of unrelieved brickwork and unbroken sheets of plate glass. However the essential strategic moves to relate it to its site seem to have been made quite effortlessly, for only on looking at the site plan does one discover how much bigger it is than the Old Palace which it extends. This building is a vivid reminder of how much better it is to get the strategic issues right without aiming at the kind of stylistic continuity which is now fashionable, but which all too often compromises and confuses the historic identity of the older building.

ABK have taken the social programme of their buildings very seriously: at the Oxford Chaplaincy much trouble was taken over the so-called narthex, a foyer space between entrance and formal meeting rooms designed to promote hospitality. Similarly, it is no surprise to find a vigorous expression of the idea of 'open school' at their Eastfield primary school in Leicestershire, but the openness is tempered by the creation of small-scale 'places' with which the child can identify. When designing a factory for Cummins at Shotts in Scotland, ABK went out of their way to consult the workforce; and when developing housing at Basildon they commissioned a social survey on the use of the shared spaces they had designed. On this worthy but mundane project the AJ commented; 'It will not attract Nikon-bearing architectural students from the ends of the earth; it is too plainly sensible for that and, of course, it is not perfect. The sad thing is that such a thorough and systematic approach is so rare'.

ABK demonstrated once again both their contextual skill and their ability with an awkward brief when they won first prize in the National Gallery extension competition of 1982. This should have taken them to the peak of their career, but instead the dream became a nightmare. First, instead of going ahead with their design as it stood, the Gallery trustees asked them to amend it, and being good social architects, ABK complied. These 'improvements' only weakened the main concept, the worst being the elimination of the proposed curved gallery around the circular courtyard which was to have been the focus of the whole. Every hope of finally building the project was dashed, however, by the Prince of Wales, when in his famous Hampton Court speech he publicly condemned the design as 'a carbuncle on the face of a well-loved friend'. As a result of this outburst, ABK lost not only that job, but other potential commissions as well. It seems ironic that the Prince with all his commendation of 'community architecture' should have failed to realise that he was dealing such a damaging blow to a firm highly regarded not just for the quality of their work, but also for their social commitment.

It will be better for posterity to judge whether ABK's proposal for the National Gallery would have been better than the design by Robert Venturi which won the second competition. What is clear already is the drastic change which has swept through British architecture: not a single competitor dared submit what could be termed a

Modernist scheme, and none tried to present a museum concept which broke with the nineteenth Century convention of toplit rectangular rooms in sequence. Historic styles broke out in kitsch combinations, and after the Prince's speech, some reference to the Classical front of the mother building seems to have become compulsory. In this atmosphere, Robert Venturi, old hand at Mannerist games with borrowed history, seemed a natural winner. Being a symmetrical building, the old National Gallery could not just be extended with more of the same, so Venturi has extended its vocabulary in his new facade in a playful and ironic way, making this intention abundantly clear. Just how such historicising with a nod and a wink will look in twenty years is hard to imagine, but the drawings and model of ABK's scheme will be there for comparison, and will surely remain a landmark in the history of British architecture.

As the debate about what buildings should look like intensifies, our attention is unfortunately diverted from the real underlying forces which make them the way they are. There is a danger that architecture will be reduced to a mere image-making role, while technical and economic forces continue to ravage the landscape undisturbed. The architect's task is getting ever more complex and more difficult and the work of ABK is a good barometer of this because they are a pragmatic firm who attempt to make the best of whatever circumstances they find themselves in. Thus typically, ABK are trying their hardest to tame the nucleus hospital system with their St Mary's hospital, Isle of Wight, at a time when many architects consider hospitals a lost cause – lost to technicalities, bureaucratic requirements, and the quantitative thinking which took over in the sixties. While making architecture out of this unpromising material, they are also breaking new ground in energy conservation. ABK can be found battling on another front at Kingston, where they have designed a massive retail development for John Lewis, taking on all the problems of scale and servicing, the confusions which arise with loss of traditional fronts and backs, and so on. If such projects lack the elegant simplicity of the Trinity Library, it is surely not because ABK have lost their touch; rather that the conditions in which their architecture can be made, always limited, have become rare.

Life goes on after the carbuncle incident, and happily ABK have not lost their nerve. Nor, in their late fifties, have the three founding partners lost their taste for innovation. With a recent small-scale project in Dorset they have been exploring an unusual technology; building with small-diameter timber. The large sawn trees normally used in construction take a long time to grow and are becoming scarcer, while young wood taken as thinnings which is too small for the sawmill is often thrown away or used for fuel. Harnessing this material is desirable from an economic viewpoint, but also because it represents a renewable resource. The new Hooke Park College therefore decided to set an example by using the material for their own buildings, with ABK as designers, Buro Happold as engineer and Frei Otto as consultant.

The trees must be used round and uncut for maximum strength, and in special structures which exploit their resistative qualities. The result is a strangely rustic architecture with roofs in sweeping curves, but involving sophisticated calculations and an elaborate jointing system. It is a far cry from the machine image of today's Hi-tech architecture, to which ABK have at times contributed, yet it may prove to be of increasing relevance as we move into the increasingly green-minded decade of the nineties. The combination of social, ideological, and technical concerns in a project like this, producing a new and unexpected architectural image, shows ABK at their best.

Wave Upon Wave

(Snatches of a conversation between an architect
and another swimmer on a beach)

Peter Ahrends

Architecture surrounds us in the news these days exerting new pressures as the media exposure intervenes and perhaps elevates the activities more publicly. What do you feel about recent events?

Perhaps it's fortuitous that we find ourselves moving along the water's edge, soft sand beneath our feet and the liquid blue of the water in contrast to the solid security of land forms, fields, isolated buildings, paths, roads, settlements and, in the depth of our unconscious, the imprint of our collective home, the structure and fabric of cities. Compellingly I remain drawn by the power of ambiguities to the study of edges particularly those which seem to move almost imperceptibly. The ebb and flow...

But what has this to do with architecture?

... almost everything in the construction of architectural ideas has to do with the delineation and illumination of...

Yes, buildings obviously have walls, windows and roofs which have edges; properties have fences, parks have clear boundaries. Even whole districts are defined by certain physical characteristics. Basic territorial stuff, isn't it?

I think that we can move far beyond territory into an area which touches upon not only the construction of the physical edge, but equally at a more abstract level the nature of ideas which are given form by the conjunction of theoretical edges, conjunctions which may be described in the medium of an architectural language.

What do you mean? Why not give an example?

Yes, let's draw here in the sand. Not the most precise way of representing ideas graphically but not uninteresting; in time the action of water and wind will erase the image, returning the beach to its natural state like sand castles transformed by erosion...

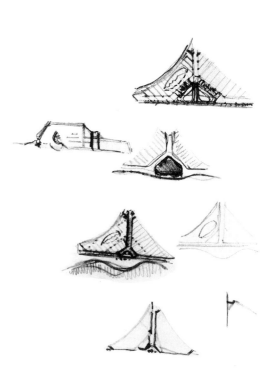

Some years ago we were asked to prepare a development plan for a new museum for the hull and artefacts of the Mary Rose, Henry VIII's sunken flagship, which were recovered from the bottom of the Solent where they had been conserved in the fine silt of the seabed since 1545.

The museum was to have three major parts. First, the Visitor Services which in addition to the main entrance concourse included elements such as a lecture theatre, a cafeteria and restaurant, a bookshop and...

Second, the main element of the Ship Hall containing the hull and a display of artefacts ranging from cannons to combs. Finally there was a series of spaces given over to conservation, research and storage, the bits behind the scene.

In thinking about the history of Henry VIII's sunken ship which sailed from the shelter of Portsmouth Harbour to confront the French Navy, I came to feel that the organisation of the plan should reflect the conjunction of three ideas, or rather three lines of movement which had a clear conceptual relevance ... Is this of interest?

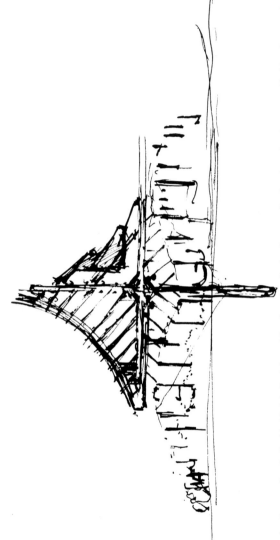

I hadn't realised that architects do more than tell the builders how to make the walls and the rooms, you know, the staircases, floors and all the other bits.

Yes, but it's not only what you 'tell the builder to make' but also the content of the ideas which serve as a conceptual framework from, say, the smallest of projects, like a piece of furniture right through to the grandeur of the anatomy of cities.

You're drifting into the structure of cities – interesting perhaps but surely of no direct relevance to the point that you were beginning to make about the Mary Rose? You were going to explain the significance of some lines which...

Yes, I hope it will become clear. There were also other complexities that I won't touch upon now. Let's just look at these three alignments. They introduce a number of ideas which are not unrelated to the stream of inventions in the Modern Movement.

Is this moving into Art History? Not my subject although I feel a strong affinity to modern images and forms without quite knowing why. I'm not sure what you're saying; is it something to do with life as we live it now ... a kind of dynamic pulse?

That's what I want to illustrate by drawing this scheme. Let's go back to the 'lines of movement' which constitute the structure of the plan.

First, this gently curved line lies parallel to the edge of the shore and serves to connect us along the water's edge from Portsmouth Harbour, the ship's birthplace, right through the building plan to the furthest point of the island of Portsmouth which is marked by this eighteenth century Ravelin Fort. The line also represents a form of movement which, as it happens, we're following as we walk along the beach, a kind of relaxed easy stroll along the edge. Not a directed line of movement but one in which we find our own pace in a re-creational sort of way. No compulsion. By contrast...

Hang about! I have the feeling that you're describing a line of force that somehow represents or connects with the unconscious. Does that have meaning? And is it so?

Yes, it has meaning but I had not intended it to have that significance. And yet...

Well, what about the other lines then?

This second stroke makes of the diagram a kind of cruciform. This was not intended to have any religious connotations but rather to represent a contradistinctive form of movement, an alignment which was intended to signify the movement of the ship as it sailed out from the safety of its harbour to engage in a violent confrontation with the French Navy off the Isle of Wight. It was in every sense an alignment that carried a different significance: an imperative, control and order in the defense of the realm.

But you've chosen to describe a very ancient sign, the cruciform which, in Christianity, has powerful symbolic meaning: perhaps the connection between that which lies above with...

I was not concerned with such readings but rather by what you said earlier about a certain dynamic which we experience in modern life. In this case the crossing of two lines serves conceptually not only as an axial and geometric framework but also as a mark of perceptual experience which was intended to be above all profoundly secular.

Maybe . . . maybe. But what's this third alignment about? This diagonal line, it doesn't seem to figure in what you've said.

The diagonal is first a discrete axis along which the hull of the Mary Rose is aligned with its bow 'pointing' to its burial place beneath the waters of the Solent. The ship is thus given its own clear presence as a reconstituted artefact of war. It also 'touches' and therefore joins the other two axes and in so doing makes a symbolic connection by linking two 'dimensions' of life that seem often to be kept apart by describing a three-dimensional figure: the right-angled triangle.

Is that all that the scheme was about? It seems so theoretical and geometric. What about the materials; and what would it have looked like? Isn't that what architecture is about, in the end?

It's about many things . . . I am trying here to describe the structure of spatial experience in this project. It's something to do with making structural volumes which sing and the way in which light makes magic of forms on the substance of their surface; and how we might, through architecture, come to appreciate new-made dimensions of our late twentieth century life; dimensions that will be 'seen' as a fabric which whilst not disconnected with the stuff of yesterday make clear contributions to our new culture. In doing so we help to construct a spirit of an age for today and tomorrow. It is the dynamic of this representation in the materiality of architecture that has meaning for me, making buildings that . . .

You still haven't explained why your buildings look as they do. There is all this talk about a return to Victorian values and the Classical Revivalists seem to be gaining ground.

A temporary aberration; a loss of nerve. Those who now take refuge in the past will come to find that this is a futile dead end rather than a useful and creative model for society now. By contrast the 'construction' of a different future offers boundless hope in a spirit of optimism and strength.

I don't know. People feel at home with what they know. The new stuff seems to have no meaning . . . no sense of comfort; there is nothing there that one can identify with.

Is there not a relationship, for instance, between the broad structural pattern of our lives and what you have described as an architecture without comfort?

Don't know . . . I haven't thought about it in this way before.

Shall we walk on? There are, if you like, one or two other ideas that we could discuss along these lines.

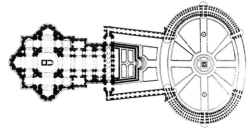

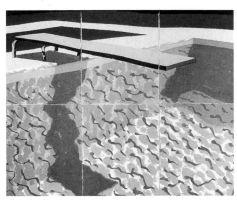

Yes, why not tell me about your partnership's scheme for the National Gallery; you know…

I was going to give that a miss if only because the Prince Charles connection has become such stereotyped media material. Mean epithets such as 'carbuncle' or 'glass stump' are used as emotional smoke screens which mask the importance of intellectual inquiry.

But why not relate aspects of what you were doing in your Gallery schemes with what you began to say about the pattern of our lives; broad ideological questions perhaps?

Here on the beach on a hot summer's morning?

Then let's go back to something else that you touched on without explanation; something to do with those alignments and their relation to … was it aspects of the Modern Movement?

Sounded pompous perhaps but there is, I think, a clear distinction to be made. Look first at the generative lines, the axes which give absolute order to the geometries of major historic buildings. Axial and often symmetrical compositions speak about completeness, order, and the representation of the perfect state of an Absolute. Compare this with the generative lines in the composition of modern work. More often than not, we find not only a representation of a dynamic which is inherently imperfectable but, importantly, compositional arrangements which move beyond the historic conventions of axes and instead refer to social, programmatic and contextual 'dimensions'.

This modern consciousness of social purpose serves to inform the volumetric and geometric dispositions of the buildings. And it is made explicit in the materiality of constructed surfaces. The interweaving of abstract facets of life take their place metaphorically in the compositional anatomy of a piece of work. These are fundamentally modern readings of an architecture which proposes a different (and ever-changing) view from the old orders which inevitably serve to carry and reaffirm archaic meanings. These are neither dead nor meaningless; but now we live elsewhere in a different world which is ours to shape.

You speak about interweaving and perhaps condensation; this suggests that there is an elaborate exchange taking place, an exchange which is difficult to tie down. Abstractions which are apparently given new form in the process of design appear to be in a state of movement.

Two thoughts come to mind: First, a short comment by the Spanish poet Lorca who said that 'all our Art is but water drawn from the well of the people; let us give it back to them in a cup of gold so that in drinking they may see themselves'. This seems to celebrate the central significance of cultural exchange as a structural proposition in Art.

Secondly, I have a visual image etched in my mind of waves upon waves upon waves. Looking down into the clear shallow water we see first the moving waved surface of the sea casting shadows which form a second reflected set of apparently different shadow-wave patterns. These in turn fall upon the third element, the wave-formed rippled surface of the sand. The eye moves easily from the separated images of any one of these parts to a view of the almost magical, interactive and dynamic movement which makes the image whole: light, shade, colour, form, liquid and solid, all apparently in a coherent state of movement.

Poetic images; but why not describe how these observations are 'reflected' in the design of one or other of your buildings? I mean why not take an example of a basic building type . . . factories?

There is a connection to be made with our design for the Cummins Engine factory at Shotts where the building consists of a number of related contiguous sheds containing a variety of sequential manufacturing functions. The diagram of the anatomy is like this.

So there is, in simplified form, a flow of materials which come into the building at one end, are machined and assembled into diesel engines which are tested and shipped out at the other end?

Yes, essentially a linear flow of product which is, however, crossed at a higher level by access routes into the building in these 'interface' spines which lie between adjacent sheds. These are also the positions of the main services plantrooms at roof level whilst at the shop floor level there is a linear zone of lockers, vending areas, notices and toilets. There is a kind of integration and overlap in these intensified areas where there are patterns of both movement and rest: a street-like character along whose length a variety of functions rub shoulders and contribute to the making of the wholeness of the place.

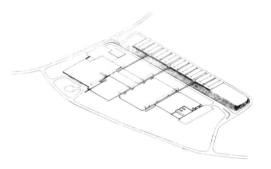

That all seems very different from the angular expression of an almost 'wavy' outside edge where the windows, wall and steel structure seem to be formed to make a series of bays. What's all that about?

There were functional reasons: for instance the break-up and absorption of the process-generated noise making comfortable conditions for the machinists. But the formal statement goes beyond this functional base into a social dimension of industrial work-patterns.

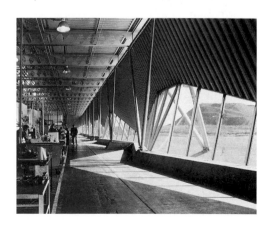

Each project offers opportunities to explore and develop agendas which aren't written down in a brief. At Shotts we were deeply involved in the formulation of the brief and amongst other studies we were instrumental in setting up a professionally conducted survey of the workers' attitudes to their place of work. Information was gathered which helped to give new direction to the social and ideological dimension of the brief.

Many of the machine workers used to bring their sandwich lunches (their 'piece'), and sit around in groups amidst the machines during the lunch break in spite of subsidised canteen food. So these outer bay-like edges (we talked earlier about the waves' edge) made places where such gatherings could naturally occur.

I had idealised fantasies of decentralised catering facilities which might in time come to serve the workforce in these populated edges where people would be seated

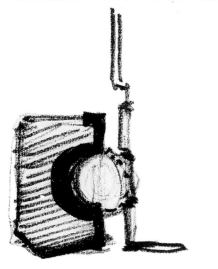

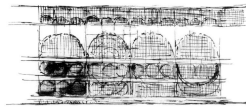

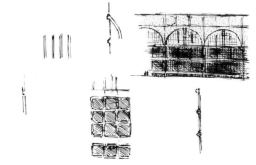

almost 'within' the new-made landscape of 'nature' outside whilst remaining in touch with the industrial world of their making inside. You can speculate about ambiguities if not contradictions.

It wouldn't take a lot of imagination to see how, under differently structured work conditions...

This sounds, as you say, idealistic if not fanciful in a fiercely competitive industrial world. Were there other aspects of the design that figured in your minds but that were never made explicit? I have the feeling that there are aspirations that underlie the conceptual work of design that may be neither fully realised or even understood?

In making architecture you are bound to work within ambiguities and contradictions which are apparent in relation to divided sets of values; a reflection of the confrontations of different worlds. Increasingly the particular orientation of commercialism which now so clearly dominates the economic structure of our lives consumes voraciously and at great speed the very aspirations which demand time and care to become ... We can't condone these conditions; nor should we be surprised to find that there are so few examples of creative excellence.

It is often said that time is money. Time is no such thing. Time may help to serve us in our search for coherent aspirations and visions that may come to contribute towards the structure of our lives. Such contributions as we are able to make in architecture will largely depend on the extent to which our ideas will bring new meaning into the making of cities. This you cannot successfully do when surrounded by the carelessness of a greed-laden culture.

Does this bring us back almost full circle to your contribution to ABK's first National Gallery scheme, and the conditions under which this was abandoned?

If you like. I don't want to hark back to the messy political dimension of the event. But we could look at some of the underlying ideas for the scheme which the Gallery were unable to accept.

They wanted something more traditional?

The Trustees were unclear and held widely differing views.

But how does this touch upon the making of cities or the double standard that you raised?

What you call the double standard was abundantly clear in the competition brief: for example, the world of fine art, the invaluable Early Renaissance collection being upheld, literally, by the commercial dimension of a property transaction. A modern concept which typifies the eighties?

No, old as the hills.

Quite. Seemed like an interesting opportunity to make a building that explored this, the blatant contradictions of the relationship, 'satisfying' each part with clarity and, we hoped, with imagination whilst also saying something about the need for a coherent formation of elements within the broader context of the city. We hoped to add to a carefully wrought piece offering a new dimension to an old place.

Rogers in his scheme physically separated these two elements. ABK not only brought them together but also shaped the whole to make an urban place?

The almost-circular court which was divided by a pedestrian route, not only made a quiet but clearly described ante-chamber in relation to the spatial progression northwards from Trafalgar Square but offered the Gallery a 'long room' whose sweeping movement was intended to be contrapuntal in relation to the rectilinear galleries which formed the outer edge. Here too was a representation of inner and outer worlds. I felt that the circular plan of the court should be geometrically incomplete; a certain open-ended dynamic was co-terminus with a new entrance stair. But we hadn't reckoned that the state of incompletion would be quite so absolute.

Obsessed by ambiguities? And cycles of incompletion?

Aren't these cycles manifestations of our internal conversations which tend to oscillate between rationality and irrationality, between our powers of analysis and the perceptions of our intuition?

Interactions between conscious and unconscious minds?

These two at least. Think of the city and the house, society and the individual. The image of the double megalith offers indescribable depth of meaning, whilst the interval of space between polarities speaks about a vibrant tranquility.

They walk on in silence for a while.

Have we reached any conclusions?

We've moved on a little.

Drink – or swim?

Yes.

September 1989

PS:
Having written this piece I later came upon an essay entitled *Reading a Wave* by Italo Calvino in his book *Mr Palomar*. He says it all in a few words. But then he knew how to write and to think:

'Mr Palomar sees a wave rise in the distance, grow, approach, change form and colour, fold over itself, break, vanish and flow again. At this point he could convince himself that he has concluded the operation he had set out to achieve, and he could go away. But it is very difficult to isolate one wave, separating it from the wave immediately following it, which seems to push it and at times overtakes it and sweeps it away; just as it is difficult to separate that one wave from the wave that precedes it and seems to drag it toward the shore, unless it turns against its follower as if to arrest it. Then if you consider the breadth of the wave, parallel to the shore, it is hard to decide where the advancing front extends regularly and where it is separated and segmented into independent waves, distinguished by their speed, shape, force and direction.'

In other words, you cannot observe a wave without bearing in mind the complex features that concur in shaping it and the other, equally complex ones that the wave itself originates. These aspects vary constantly, so each wave is different from another wave, even if not immediately adjacent or successive; in other words there are some forms and sequences that are repeated. though irregularly distributed in space and time.

P.A.

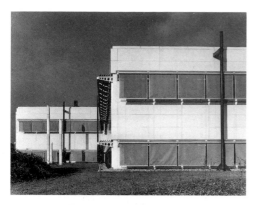

leaving open-ended situations to deal with future change. In the case of Cummins, it meant allowing for a change of fuel and we left enough site area for coal hoppers and coal delivery to the Energy centre which were subsequently installed when a decision to change to coal was made.

Another building, an office for W. H. Smith at Swindon (p. 138), successfully achieved energy savings using natural ventilation and solar shading in relation to deepish office space. This is an important development at a time when many health problems are occurring in deep artificially ventilated offices. The aesthetic effect was marked both externally and internally; externally with automatic blinds set well away from the building to provide shading but also to allow ventilation and internally by exposing the coffered concrete ceilings to provide heat storage to smooth out daily temperature swings, thus keeping the building comfortable.

Our major energy conserving building is St. Mary's Hospital, Newport, Isle of Wight (p. 128). The building is planned to use 50% less energy than a normal modern hospital by means of a series of interrelated measures. It is as far as possible naturally ventilated and naturally lit. The natural lighting is enhanced by planning the wards on upper floors and giving them top light. The whole fabric of the building is well insulated and airproofed and consideration has been given to patient comfort as a means to obviate the need for excess temperatures and thus the use of unnecessary energy in winter. Heat recovery in the hospital with the re-use of energy for low temperature requirements is considerable. Energy management techniques with feedback to staff of their resulting success or failure on a comparative basis have been studied. In addition the landscape has been developed with James Hope and Eddie Fairfield to shelter the hospital from inhospitable winds by means of tree belts so that the temperatures in the courtyards in autumn, winter and spring can be significantly higher than surrounding air temperatures leading to more actual use of the courts and less heat loss from surrounding facades.

Our approach to energy here is to use a collection of known and tried techniques and to relate them in such a way that they save energy and thus money but also create aesthetic and social opportunities. The building will be a better place, more comfortable and interesting to be in with its internal forms modulated by the constantly changing quality of natural light such that the people who will use it will be the beneficiaries.

Feedback as to how well architects have succeeded in providing what their clients' requirements demand usually depends on rumour, journalistic reaction or catastrophe to the great detriment of architectural progress. The need for feedback was pointed out to me in 1973 by Beryl Geber, then a lecturer at the London School of Economics in social psychology. She also suggested that the practice take on Peter Ellis, the best student of that year, to work with us. Peter was with us for three years, during which time the foundations were laid for proper evaluation and feedback methods from local authority housing. The evaluations we did had the merit of being done on the same estate, Chalvedon, Basildon, over three years with the same people interviewed three times. Architects were involved with Peter carrying out the work and this led to 'constant feedback'. However, the main conclusions of the first deep survey were so clear that we were able to change the overall planning of the layout of later stages of the scheme. In addition, we as architects were able to get answers to questions by means of quick surveys which we required when designing the details of the housing.

Significantly our rapport with the tenants became close and in 1974 Basildon Corporation asked us to design a Community Centre with the tenants as our clients. This was our first brush with what has since become known as 'Community Architecture' and a precursor of briefing techniques in that subject. Suffice to say the result is immensely popular. This form of briefing developed by ourselves and others at the time and which includes feedback has fundamentally effected the way housing is tackled in this country.

The design of a factory for Cummins Engines was also preceeded by a survey of worker requirements and complaints about the existing plant. This led to considerable attention being paid by us to the planning of the eating facilities in a central position in the plan and attention to sound attenuation which significantly effected the design of the external walls.

It has been said that briefing is of utmost importance; my view is that without feedback it is often theoretical. It is for that reason we, and other architects, together set up Building Use Studies which is a research organisation to monitor interactive feedback. It has done significant work in the field of Energy Conservation, Sick-Building Syndrome, the causes of Vandalism in schools and has proved that it is the interactive nature of buildings, equipment and people that causes the problems and opportunities.

There is no doubt that one of the most important ingredients in a total approach to architecture is the group of elements which bridge between the utilitarian and the higher aspects of man. These are the elements which extend meaning or symbolise a world that could be and additionally they satisfy a need in man for sensory stimulation and pleasure. I speak of art, craft and decoration. As architects our role is to integrate those elements harmoniously whether we or others have created them. Today we are seeing a demand for their reintegration and therefore there is an opportunity to make a valuable and lasting contribution to this perennial problem in our own way, relating to our time and to the enormous talent locked up in the artists, craftsmen and designers of our era. Five of our schemes are particularly relevant. The Library (p. 36) and Arts Building at Trinity College Dublin (p. 87) where sculpture, wallhangings and painting abound side by side with our sculptural approach to space, they are treated as objects in that space. I am struck by the way the Calder stabile elegantly holds its place in the large Fellows Square and the golden Pomodoro sets off the grey forecourt of the Library so well. Each are objects to take the eye and give it pleasure and yet leave a question in the mind. Internally the influence of George Dawson can be seen, his inspiration gave the Arts Building the Douglas Hyde art gallery whilst the building's walls became resting places for the National Collection of Modern Art with Scott, Lichtenstein and others. The Irish are visually aware and adventurous in a way the English need to become.

The second building is Templeton College, Oxford (p. 55), in which a quiet revolution took place. In 1968 the College decided to employ two little known craftsmen, John Makepeace and Ann Sutton, to work with us on the furniture and fittings of the residential building. The rooms that resulted were and are simple yet with that special quality that comes from the application of good design and excellent craftsmanship.

The building has since received the work of many craftsmen and artists and has shown how such work can be well integrated with modern architecture. Fred Baier's

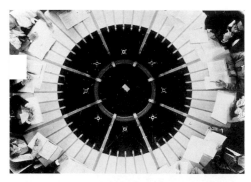

table for our 'Thinking Room' was the result of the first limited craftsman competition, since carried out with such success nationally. The table is memorable for its design and quality and the room is special because of the way the architecture and the piece respond to each other. It also happens to work very well as a table and is beautifully made.

James Hope's pyramid of plants and Hugh Scriven's furniture join together with John Makepeace's original periodical racks to create a library/information centre in which people enjoy to work and which symbolically represents the importance of information in the management process both by its position and distinctive quality.

At Habitat in Wallingford (p. 95), Terence Conran commissioned Paolozzi to create some outstanding play sculptures. Because of the sensitivity of the artist they stand in harmony with the building and functionally are also extremely successful.

W. H. Smith's Headquarters at Swindon contrasts building, landscape and sculpture to produce a long and interesting approach to the building keeping the eye involved with Elizabeth Frink's figures humorous in their comment on 'haste'. Internally Sally Freshwater has done a delicate hanging, again very much in tune with the architecture. In St. Mary's Hospital I.O.W. all the mentioned techniques have been brought together and many methods of achieving the fusion of art and craft in a modern bulding have been evolved and applied. In addition live art such as music, story telling and drama have been given their place in the overall plan.

Landscape with the theme of water has been developed by James Hope to provide fine views and places to visit in the grounds. The lake makes reference to Monet's garden, creating a world within the world in which patients, staff and the public can regenerate themselves. The internal courts all interpret the theme of water either actively or as in the case of the dry river bed court passively. Inside the building Candice Bahouth has designed an embroidered hanging for the main stair, made of 120 squares, each square is being made by a different person or group on the island. A piece of community art. Stuart Hill, a blacksmith, has devised the lily seat for the outpatients' courtyard. Distinguished sculptors such as Bill Pye and Liliane Lijn are working with us.

This is the first National Health Hospital to plan for art and craft from its inception and this in itself has liberated incipient talent and given the many members of the client body a real feeling of participation. Since starting the project, research information has confirmed the commonsense view that stimulating surroundings can improve patient recovery in a number of ways. Further, the morale of the staff has been, and also will be, improved by such manifestations which are a necessary balance to a scientific/medical milieu.

So we have come full circle and find that in our energy-conserving hospital using the latest technology, the social and healing activities are benefitted by art and craft created in harmony with architecture.

This building is an example of where refuge in the past has been eschewed for the opportunities of the present based on the 'perennial principle' to the benefit of all who use it in the future.

Architecture or Appearances

Some thoughts from the drawing board

Paul Koralek

It seems to me that there is so much confusion and such diversity of opinion about directions in Architecture – indeed about the very nature of Architecture – that it is necessary to try to re-examine the basis on which we are trying to work, the principles underlying our work and how we understand our objectives.

In spite of increasing public interest and the resulting controversy there is not enough discussion or consideration of such questions. It is perhaps not surprising in an age dominated by communication and the communication 'media' that appearances, 'style' or 'image' should become all important. Not surprising that opinion and taste should be moulded by journalists and commentators rather than those engaged in the process of Architecture. Fashions come and go with alarming rapidity.

The last thirty years have seen an enormous amount of new building. The quality of much of this is appalling and not surprisingly there has been a widespread reaction. Ironically perhaps this has given rise to a growing interest in Architecture and an increasing awareness of the quality of the built environment and its effect on many aspects of our lives. The resultant debate however seems largely to concern questions of 'style' or appearances and is presented very largely in terms of Tradition versus Modernism, a naive and superficial view which begs the questions of what a living tradition is and how to establish a real relationship with it. Architecture is seen in terms of simple alternatives – functional or pleasurable, rational or emotional, classical or romantic. Why this simplistic juxtaposition, this kind of 'either or'? These things are not incompatible unless we make them so. Architecture involves the reconciliation of these apparent opposites.

Architecture should not be a question of whether or not we put Corinthian capitals onto our facades. It is about people and their lives; about making spaces that will have a living, dynamic and significant relationship with the life and activity they will contain.

It is very disturbing to me that the debate is conducted at such a superficial level – that an essentially superficial view of Architecture – a view concerned only with the superficial, the surface, should predominate. This is a trivialisation of Architecture. Architecture is surely more important and more difficult than that.

The question of appearance – or appearances – is essentially superficial. This is not to say that it is unimportant – of course it is important and architects would be the first to recognise this – but it is essentially secondary. When it becomes primary the process of design is turned upside down and we lose sight of any reaonable or meaningful sense of values or purpose. Architecture is not primarily about appearances. It is about making buildings and places for people to live and work in. First of all it is about making these buildings in an intelligent, economical and efficient manner; in a manner that will withstand the ravages of use – and misuse – of time and climate. It is about making buildings that will provide a comfortable and healthy physical environment both inside and out. But above all, it is about creating an environment that is satisfying to all aspects of a human being; the physical, the psychological and the spiritual. To my mind there is no essential conflict or contradiction between these different aspects or objectives although some are much more subtle and complex than others and they involve a continuous relative evaluation and an assessment of priorities in each particular case. The same considerations apply over a very wide range of scales, from a tiny detail to an entire city. The larger scale of course involves wider social and economic considerations.

A city responds to the social and economic pressures of our particular society. The relative importance of our social institutions constantly changes. There are vast contradictions between a predominantly materialistic outlook and the resultant commercialism and tendency towards growth, leading to an ever increasingly large scale, on the one hand; and, on the other, a yearning for a more comprehensible environment with institutions at a more intimate and 'human' scale, within a framework that reflects their true relationships. There are inherent conflicts between such contrasting requirements as mobility and security, permanence and flexibility, enclosure and openess, intimacy and grandeur.

Our evaluation and response to such considerations and our understanding and application of the available techniques and methods of construction will determine the kind of buildings we produce. If we use steel and glass – without disguising them – it is called 'Hi tech'. If we use brick and tile it is called 'vernacular' but surely it is a question not of one thing or the other but of using appropriate technologies. 'Hi-tech' is no more or less rational than any other technology. Neither is it any more or less romantic. Of course there are many other factors and considerations which mould the form of a building, not least a sensitivity to context and an appropriateness to a particular location, a sense of place. In some cases this may be the dominant consideration; but important as it is it is only one aspect among many. It must not be forgotten that buildings are for people and that they are to be lived in and used. That they serve human and social functions – both practical and spiritual. That they exist in order to accommodate, enhance and enrich the life and activity that they will contain, to satisfy the needs of the psyche as well as physical needs. The distinction between these different categories of needs may be convenient – but it is nevertheless artificial and misleading. We cannot really separate them – indeed I think that they stand in a subtle and complex interrelationship, and that Architecture is concerned with just this interrelationship.

It is easy to speak of the needs of the psyche, but much more difficult to know what they are. We can only really know them in ourselves, and know perhaps more easily when they are unfulfilled. But it is clear that a purely, or excessively, intellectual approach can obscure the issue and all too easily misinterpret our real needs. In recent years Architecture has clearly failed in many respects, to meet people's real needs. Most urban housing and speculative office buildings bear witness to this. But even though we can recognise the failures or our profession and learn from the mistakes of the last thirty years, it is more difficult to draw the right conclusions: The results are too often condemned without any understanding of the reasons for the underlying dissatisfaction. The sheer barreness, boredom and squalor of most of the building of the last thirty years is simplistically attributed to 'modernism' and 'functionalism' without any real consideration of what this means. It has therefore become somewhat unfashionable to talk of function and functionalism. This is seen as a kind of moral or moralistic approach. It has however nothing to do with morality and I am convinced that the ideas behind what is called 'Functionalism' lie at the root of the question of design. These ideas are important and go far beyond a mere utilitarianism. They go far beyond style and fashion. I think that they are timeless and that they involve fundamental principles that underlie all true architecture. Functionalism is not a 'style' – it is an essential aspect or principle of Architecture.

The aims of the Bauhaus, which exerted so seminal an influence on the development of Modern Architecture, were, in the words of Walter Gropius: '. . . not to propagate any 'style', system or dogma but simply to exert a revitalising influence on design.' Le Corbusier, too, made the point that 'Architecture has nothing in common with styles'. I would add the words of the Art Historian, Ananda Coomeraswamy: 'Styles are the accident, by no means the essence of art.'

A style, in fact, is the result of a way of working and grows out of a whole complex of ideas and attitudes and in the past from a language of symbolism which had its roots in religion and which relates to techniques of craftsmanship and methods of construction.

So a style cannot simply be put on like a suit of clothes. That is to belittle it to the level of fashion, or worse still a game. Real architecture cannot deal with mere appearances, it concerns itself with reality and with meaning, and the face it presents to the world must be a reflection of this reality. If not, it becomes a stage set: a world of make-believe which is shallow, superficial and ultimately deeply dissatisfying. A living relationship with a tradition is a far more subtle, difficult and rewarding matter than a mere repetition of predetermined forms. T.S. Eliot expressed this very beautifully in his essay on *Tradition and the Individual Talent*. He speaks of a vital dynamic relationship with the past – far more challenging and interesting than mere conformity and repetition; and though he was writing about literature, his words apply equally to architecture, or any art: '. . . we are aware of the leaves of a tree when the autumn wind begins to blow them off – when they have separately ceased to be vital. Energy may be wasted at that point in a frantic endeavour to collect the leaves as they fall and gum them onto the branches; but the sound tree will put forth new leaves, and the dry tree should be put to the axe. We are always in danger, in clinging to an old tradition, or attempting to re-establish one, of confusing the vital and the unessential, the real and the sentimental. Our second danger is to associate tradition with the immovable; to think of it as something hostile to all change; to aim to return to some previous condition which we imagine as having been capable of preservation in perpetuity, instead of aiming to stimulate the life which produced that condition in its time.'[1] 'Yet if the only form of tradition, of handing down, consisted in following the ways of the immediate generation before us in a blind or timid adherence to its successes, 'tradition' should positively be discouraged. We have seen many such simple currents soon lost in the sand; and novelty is better than repetition. Tradition is a matter of much wider significance. It cannot be inherited and if you want it you must obtain it by great labour . . .'[2]

This cannot be approached superficially – as it were from the outside, but only from an understanding of principles – from within. The process – or profession – of architecture becomes a search for these principles. Only when we engage in this process, which we call design, do these questions come alive and take on real meaning, as we try to re-establish and re-affirm the relationship between purpose, material and technique.

Louis Sullivan's axiom 'Form follows function' is a clear statement of a principle, an expression of the relationship between form and function which has come to be loosely described as 'Functionalism'. This concept of, and approach to, design is much misunderstood, and the word is confused with mere utilitarianism. Functionalism is not a style. Nor is it a rejection of ornament. It is an attitude to the search for form, the relationship of form to content, or meaning, which is all-embracing and can relate the many different aspects of design.

I think that the earliest statement of this concept is by Louis Sullivan, written in his book *Kindergarten Chats* published in 1896: 'All things in nature have a shape, that is to say, a form, an outward semblance that tells us what they are, that distinguishes them from ourselves and from each other. Unfailingly in nature these shapes express the inner life, the native quality ... It is the pervading law of all things organic, and inorganic, of all things physical and metaphysical, of all things human and all things superhuman, of all true manifestations of the head, of the heart, of the soul, that the life is recognizable in its expression, that form ever follows functions. This is the law'. 'Shall we then daily violate this law in our art? Are we so decadent, so imbecile, so utterly weak of eyesight that we cannot perceive this truth so simple, so very simple? Is it indeed a truth so transparent that we see through it but do not see it?'[3]

Sullivan expresses a living, vibrant two-way relationship between what for the sake of simplicity we can call 'form' and 'function'. 'Just as every form contains its function and exists by virtue of it, so every function finds or is engaged in finding its form. And furthermore, while this is true of the everyday things we see about us in nature and in the reflection of nature we call human life, it is just as true, because it is a universal law, of everything that the mind can take hold of.'[4] Sullivan is in fact speaking of the 'what-ness' of things – their 'quality'.

He goes far beyond a merely utilitarian concept of architecture. He is restating a fundamental principle. He saw function as a metaphysical concept. He speaks of 'the law' not 'a law'. He pre-supposes a universal or cosmic order, an underlying level of meaning which we can only try to approach and to that extent reflect in our work. Meaning is not something that can be fabricated. It has to be found. The word 'to invent' means 'to find', 'to come upon'. Coomeraswamy describes what he calls Traditional Art in much the same terms as Sullivan speaking of 'Modern' architecture. 'In traditional art, function and meaning are inseparable'. And, 'All possessions not at the same time beautiful and useful are an affront to human dignity. Ours is perhaps the first society to find it natural that some things should be beautiful and others useful.' ...[5]

This is not at all the same as saying that because a thing is useful it is by definition beautiful; nor is it the same as the current tendency to confuse means with ends. Technique and Technology can only be means, not ends. It is a view of functionalism which in fact includes what we call ornament. Coomeraswamy gives this definition of ornament or decoration: 'Our use of the word 'decorative' would have been abusive as if we spoke of mere millinery or upholstery; for all the words purporting decoration in many languages, (Mediaeval Latin included), referred originally not to anything that could be added to an already finished and effective product merely to please the eye or ear but to the completion of anything with whatever might be necessary to its functioning whether with respect to the mind or the body: perfection, rather than beauty, was the end in view.'[6] While Sullivan speaks of an ornamented building: 'This is to say, a building which is truly a work of art (and I consider none other) is in its nature, essence and physical being an emotional expression. This being so, and I feel deeply that it is so, it must have almost literally a life.'[7]

Understood in this way, ornament must be seen as an integral part of a building – necessary for its completion. Ornament can, as it were, stand between us and the more abstract qualities of a building – elaborating its inherent characteristics, hinting at the underlying order. The Greek word *Kosmos* signified ornament as well as order. Ornament cannot, however, replace the more fundamental aspects of a building. It must complement them. It must have its roots in the principles and techniques of the architecture itself. It cannot be applied like a cosmetic. There can be nothing whimsical or arbitrary about it. For me, the seeds of ornament are in the details of construction – an elaboration, a celebration of the process of making a building: the joints and connections, the points of support and stress in the structure, the entrances and patterns of movement, the way light enters to reveal the forms and spaces. Making virtues of necessities or taking materials or techniques to their limits. Everything becomes a question of function in the broadest sense: 'So the first sane questions that can be asked about a work of art are, 'What was it for'? and 'What does it mean'? We have seen already that whatever, and however humble the functional purpose of the work of art may have been, it had always a spiritual meaning, by no means an arbitrary meaning but one that the function itself expresses adequately by analogy. Function and meaning cannot be forced apart; the meaning of a work of art is its intrinsic form as much as the soul is the form of the body.'[8]

In contrast, so-called Post-Modernist talk about meaning and symbolism seems to me far too lightweight and superficial. We are not talking about a simplistic sign language but an integration and correspondence of all aspects of a building; a meaningful relationship that is much more difficult to find. In particular, the idea of 'symbols' and 'symbolism' is taken far too superficially. In fact this idea of symbolism refers to much deeper levels of meaning. The word comes from the Greek verb 'symballein', which means to join together. Symbolism is not merely an equivalence that can be rationalised. It is another language which does not speak only to our intellect, a perception of a correspondence of different orders of meaning. I would like to illustrate this with some quotations, which, incidentally, make it clear that a symbol too, has a function: 'Adequate symbolism may be defined as a representation of a reality on a certain level of reference by a corresponding reality on another.'[9]

'. . . the function of a symbol is precisely that of revealing a whole reality, inaccessible to other means of knowledge.'[10]

'The difference between 'symbol' and what is nowadays commonly called 'allegory' is simple to grasp. An allegory remains at the same level of evidence and perception, whereas the symbol guarantees the correspondence between two universes belonging to different levels. Symbol is the means, and the only one of penetrating into the invisible, into the world of mystery.'[11]

'Let us beware, however, of supposing that symbolism refers only to the 'spiritual' and the 'material' is without meaning; the two planes are complementary. The fact that a dwelling house is supposed to be at 'the centre of the world' does not make it any the less a convenience which answers to specific needs and is conditioned by the climate, the economic structure of society and the architectural tradition.'[12]

This perhaps brings us back to our starting point and to some of the mundane problems with which we have to deal – but also to their link with a much deeper search that finally gives meaning to our work as architects. These ideas do not deny the many technical and practical problems with which we have to deal. On the contrary, they provide a basis from which it is possible to search for coherent and integrated solutions to these problems, so that we can make buildings which will be satisfactory and fulfilling in relation to all levels and aspects of human life and activity.

1 T S Eliot 'Tradition' from 'After Strange Gods'
2 T S Eliot 'Tradition and the Individual Talent'
3 Louis Sullivan 'Kindergarten Chats'
4 Louis Sullivan 'Kindergarten Chats'
5 Ananda Coomeraswamy (Art Historian and Curator of the Museum of Oriental Art, Boston)
6 Ananda Coomeraswamy
7 Louis Sullivan 'Kindergarten Chats'
8 Ananda Coomeraswamy
9 Ananda Coomeraswamy
10 Mircea Eliade (Professor of the History of Religion, University of Chicago)
11 Henry Corbin (Professor of Islamic Religion, Sorbonne)
12 Mircea Eliade

Library forecourt

Berkeley Library, Trinity College
Dublin
1961-1967

Trinity College Library is one of the six copyright libraries in the British Isles, receiving by right a copy of every book published in Great Britain. Its intake is therefore enormous. A new building was required, as an addition to the eighteenth century Library, to accommodate the ever-growing book stock and to provide for a student population of up to 4000.

Our design for this Library was the winning entry in an international competition held in 1960. The new building was to be the first in Trinity College since the thirties and the largest since the nineteenth century. The competition brief explicitly called for a new building that would represent the twentieth century as the College's earlier buildings represented the eighteenth and nineteenth. The College required a working library that would provide reading places for 470 and book storage capacity for up to 830,000 volumes, the estimated intake for 25 years.

Our interpretation of the brief centred around two particular aspects of the new building, its relationship to the surrounding historic college buildings and the design of spaces with a character appropriate to reading and study.

Trinity College consists of a succession of courts, gardens and quadrangles, inward looking, self-sufficient, with a continuous history of several hundred years. The library site was poised between the old library designed by Thomas Burgh in 1732 – the home of the Book of Kells – and the nineteenth century Museum by Deane and Woodward,

beloved of Ruskin. It was bordered on one side by the Fellows' Garden and on the other by the open playing fields of College Park. The new building was sited to create a forecourt on a new podium between the two older buildings so that architecture representing three centuries encloses the space.

A basement level, extending under the podium and connecting with the old library, houses a vast capacity of bookstacks. The ground floor contains the catalogue and reference section, and administration areas; the first and second floors together form one large reading and open-access book storage area. The design of these two levels, with a high proportion of built-in furniture, became an exploration of the nature of study spaces, providing large and small spaces with different degrees of enclosure and contrasting qualities of light, to give choice and variety to the users.

The predominant material, inside and out, is reinforced concrete made with white cement and light coloured sand. Most of the reading spaces are top lit, but views out to the surrounding gardens and spaces are provided by storey-height bay windows made of single sheets of curved glass in bronze frames which are an important element of the exterior design, contrasting with the cubic forms of white concrete and granite of the walls.

Awards
1961 1st Prize International Competition

Client
Trinity College,
University of Dublin
Structural Engineer
F.J. Samuely & Partners
Services Engineer
Steensen Varming Mulcahy

Quantity Surveyor
D.A. Degerdon & Partners
General Contractor
G.&T. Crampton Ltd.
Area 7,115 m²

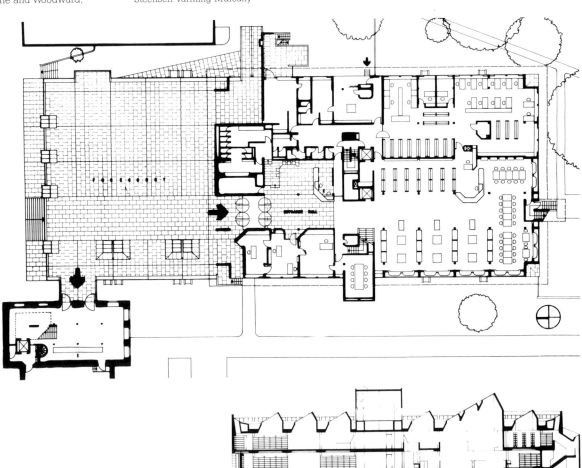

Ground floor plan

Section

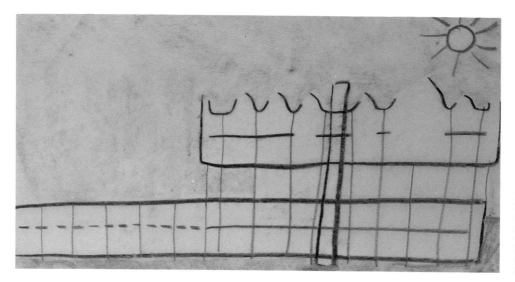

Sketch section showing rooflighting concept and division of the building into its three main parts: second level upper reading area, second level basement bookstack and ground floor admin, catalogue and reference area

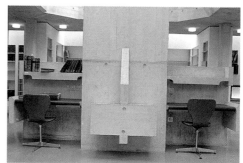

Second floor reading area with light shaft to first floor below

North elevation with main entrance and forecourt: Dean and Woodward's Museum building on the left and Thomas Burgh's library on the right

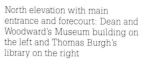

Main reading area at first floor level

Top-lit reading room

West elevation to the Fellows'
Garden (now Fellows' Square)

West elevation

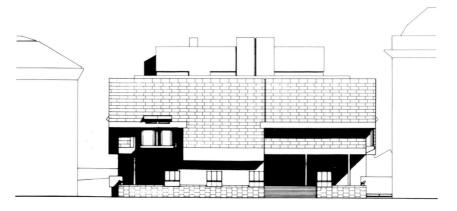

North elevation

Chichester Theological College
Sussex

Residential Building

1961-1965

On a beautiful country garden site, this building forms a link between the main College building and the Chapel. It is a natural route for people going from one to the other and affords superb views across the landscape in three directions.

The College needed a large number of study-bedrooms, some staff flats and a library and lecture room. The new building was conceived as outer 'walls' formed of the smaller elements enclosing the larger ones. Its situation between the old buildings was deliberately chosen so that the new accommodation would not become an Annexe but would integrate with the established College buildings. For this reason great emphasis was placed on the routes to and from Chapel and College through the court, and the library was included in the brief to provide a major college focus within the new building.

Small groups of study bedrooms were stepped back to create a more sheltered sense of enclosure in the court and to give double-glazed top-lighting to the individual rooms. The play of top-light and cross-light became a theme of the design – as an antidote to the flat bland lighting associated with rooms lit only from one end and differentiating between the two functions of a window: the admission of light and the provision of views out. In the study bedrooms this gave a well-lit sheltered workplace with pin-up space and bookshelves in front of the desk. Built-in furniture was specially designed by the architects to make the most of the relatively modest dimensions.

The whole building is of rugged natural materials – local brick, concrete and stained pine externally with simple white painted concrete block walls inside with colour sparingly used on pine doors stained orange, blue and yellow.

Client
Chichester Theological College

Structural Engineer
F.J. Samuely & Partners

Quantity Surveyor
E.C. Harris & Partners

General Contractor
Jno Croad Ltd

Area 1139 m^2

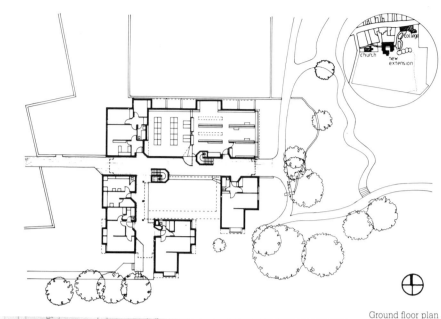

Ground floor plan

View from the south

Library interiors

The courtyard

Chichester Theological College. Typical study bedroom with rooflight over desk alcove

Kasmin Gallery

Bond Street, London

1963

In 1963 John Kasmin established a new gallery for modern British and American Art, dealing in painters such as Richard Smith, Morris Louis, and David Hockney. This design for the conversion of a small Bond Street showroom for the Kasmin Gallery was specifically for the display of such paintings. The frontage on Bond Street was minimal, a small entrance door opening onto a long, narrow, mysterious, winding corridor, where subdued light and narrow dimensions deliberately contrasted with the sudden arrival at the gallery itself: a large, high, white, top-lit space.

The quality of the design derived chiefly from the simple sculptural form of the space, the quality of light and its restrained detailing. Particularly important were the form of the section, the design of the rooflight to give controlled illumination by daylight and artificial light; smooth transitions of planes and surfaces and the profile of openings.

Client
Kasmin Ltd

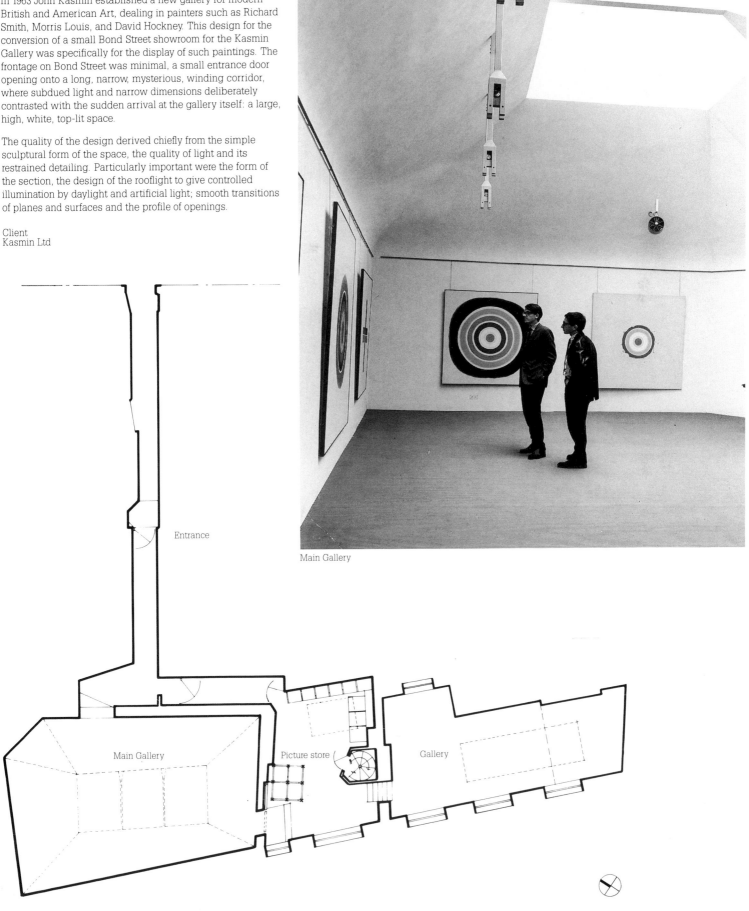

Main Gallery

Entrance

Main Gallery

Picture store

Gallery

Roman Catholic Chaplaincy
Oxford
1972

The Chaplaincy was originally housed in the beautiful seventeenth century Bishop's Palace fronting onto St. Aldates, but over the years had to make do with a number of makeshift additions. The new building was needed in order to expand the Chaplaincy's activities as the social and religious centre for Roman Catholics at the University of Oxford.

When the project started, the City had not yet developed plans for land to the south of the awkward, irregular and restricted site behind the Old Palace, which meant that the design of the Chaplaincy had to proceed in a planning vacuum without reference to its future surroundings. The site was completely filled by the new building which connected to the Bishop's Palace on three levels so that the old building was fully integrated into the new complex and would retain its place as the spiritual centre of Catholic Oxford.

The new building was organised in layers of ascending privacy, the most public being at ground level so that its very large multi-purpose hall was readily accessible and could also be hired out for various functions. This space – the Newman Room – posed particular problems of design because it had to be divisible into smaller spaces while remaining equally appropriate for secular use and for the celebration of Sunday Mass. At this 'public' level there is also a small chapel for private prayer and weekday Mass. The main entrance area, which includes a coffee bar and exhibition area, mediates between the larger congregational spaces and the Bishop's Palace.

There are more secluded but still public areas on the first floor – a library and a small meeting room – with the floors above them being the most private for study bedrooms and a residents' common room.

The difficulty of adding a relatively large new structure to the intimately scaled old building was solved by planning the smaller elements, which share an affinity of function and scale, adjacent to it. The relationship was emphasised by angled windows stepped out at each bay to echo, without imitating, the lively facade and gables of the Bishop's Palace.

Client
Trustees of the Newman Trust
Structural Engineer
F.J. Samuely & Partners
Services Engineer
Max Fordham & Partners
Quantity Surveyor
D.A. Degerdon & Partners
General Contractor
Laurence James Ltd
Area 1,488 m²

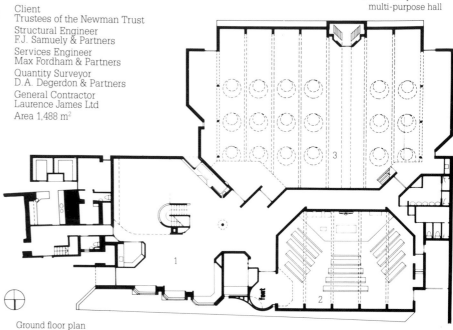

1 Entrance foyer
2 Chapel
3 Main chapel/ multi-purpose hall

Ground floor plan

The Main Chapel

View from St. Aldate's with main entrance and the old Bishop's Palace on the left

St. Anne's Church
Soho, London

Project

1964

After the Second World War, all that remained of St. Anne's Church, Soho, originally built in 1690, was the bell tower of 1802 by S. P. Cockerell. The new design aimed to harmonise with its historic background and complement the vigorous silhouette of the remaining tower.

The brief required a new church seating 250, a non-denominational chapel, sacristy, vestry, rectory, church offices, public meeting rooms and flats with a provision for 230 underground car spaces.

Partly as a consequence of the car-parking need, the structure of the church above was designed to localise the entire weight of the building on four points of support freeing the space beneath with the minimum obstruction. The interior space of the church was then defined by four reinforced concrete columns, one at the centre of each side of a square, with four open-web concrete beams spanning diagonally across the corners between them. The more delicate structure of the roof and walls was supported on this concentrated and massive framework.

The entire surface, roof and walls, was to be made of a translucent composite skin of double glazing and metal mesh with artificial ventilation in the cavity between the layers of glass. The objective was to produce a diaphanous sound-proof enclosure which would admit a soft radiant light while eliminating direct sunshine and glare. By day it would appear as a translucent skin, by night the structure within would be revealed.

Client
Rector, St. Anne's Church and
London Diocesan Fund
Structural Engineer
Charles Weiss & Partners

Services Engineer
Associated Architects &
Consultants
Quantity Surveyor
E.C. Harris & Partners

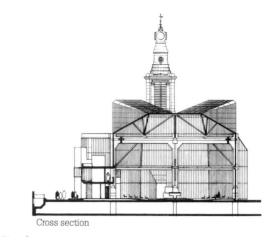

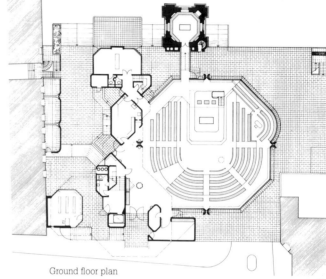

Cross section

Ground floor plan

Dunstan Road Houses
Old Headington, Oxford
1966-1969

Five individual owners joined together to form the Lower Farm Housing Group to build these private houses on the western edge of the village of Old Headington. The rural site slopes gently towards the north west with good views to the north over open countryside.

The layout gives each house a private walled garden facing south, reached from a shared garage forecourt and leading along the side of the house to more open gardens on the north which take advantage of the distant views. This establishes a sequence of increasing privacy from the public road, through the communal forecourt to the private courtyard and entry.

The houses themselves are made of concrete block cavity walls to provide an inexpensive basic shell with a minimum of applied finishes – acknowledging that the owners might wish to add to the fabric over the years. The five house plans are similar without being identical and were designed not only to take advantage of north views and south sun, but also to give each owner some choice about how the house might be used. Some opted for children's rooms, kitchen and dining room on the ground floor with living room and master bedroom above on the first floor; others adopted the more conventional arrangement of living and dining on the ground floor with bedrooms above. In keeping with the idea of a basic shell, the internal finishes are simple: painted lightweight block walls and plastered ceilings, with storey-height cladding panels incorporating sliding aluminium windows.

The scheme was completed on a very modest budget.

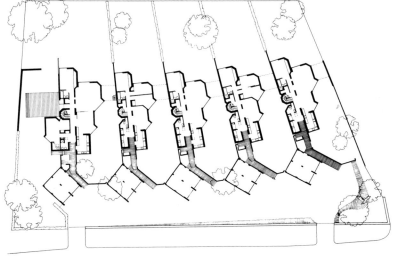

Client
The Lower Farm
Housing Group
Structural Engineer
David Powell & Partners
Quantity Surveyor
D.A. Degerdon & Partners
General Contractor
Ephraim Organ & Son Ltd.
Housing Units 5

Site layout plan

Bell Tower
Canberra

Competition Entry

1968

This design was an entry in a limited competition for a bell tower – the gift of the British Government to Australia to mark the jubilee of the founding of the federal capital. The site, a small island on a lake in a key position in the heart of Canberra, was particularly important in relation to many fine distant views from the surrounding area. The design hinged on two major and complementary aspects: its form, scale and silhouette in relation to its surroundings, and an attempt to find an appropriate twentieth century meaning for the idea of a 'monument'.

If a monument represents its time and is an expression of current values, what is its significance in an anti-monumental age? How can the virtues of permanence and stability be reconciled with the modern ethos and the dynamic quality of science and technology? How to combine the practical problem – to hold a carillon of large and heavy bells up in the air – with the symbolic need to express the motivations and aspirations of our time? The search for answers to these practical and philosophical questions led to a lively and enjoyable collaboration with the structural consultants. In one sense the structural problem really had to be invented before a solution could be found.

In the past, monumental structures relied on mass for stability, whereas now it is possible to use high-strength materials and new techniques to make very light-weight structures which achieve stability through their form and which, when viewed in motion, appear to be poised and dynamic. From a distance the twin lattices of different heights would appear as an ever-changing silhouette of diaphanous filigree screens around the central nucleus of the carillon housing. From closer, the details of the structure and connections would become evident and would provide a sense of scale and a renewed interest.

Client
Ministry of Works
Structural Engineer
Ove Arup & Partners
Quantity Surveyor
D.A.Degerdon & Partners

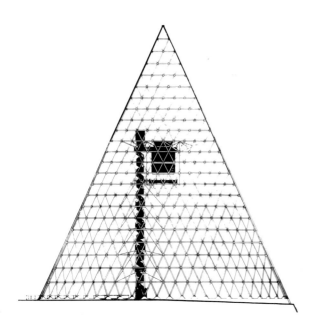

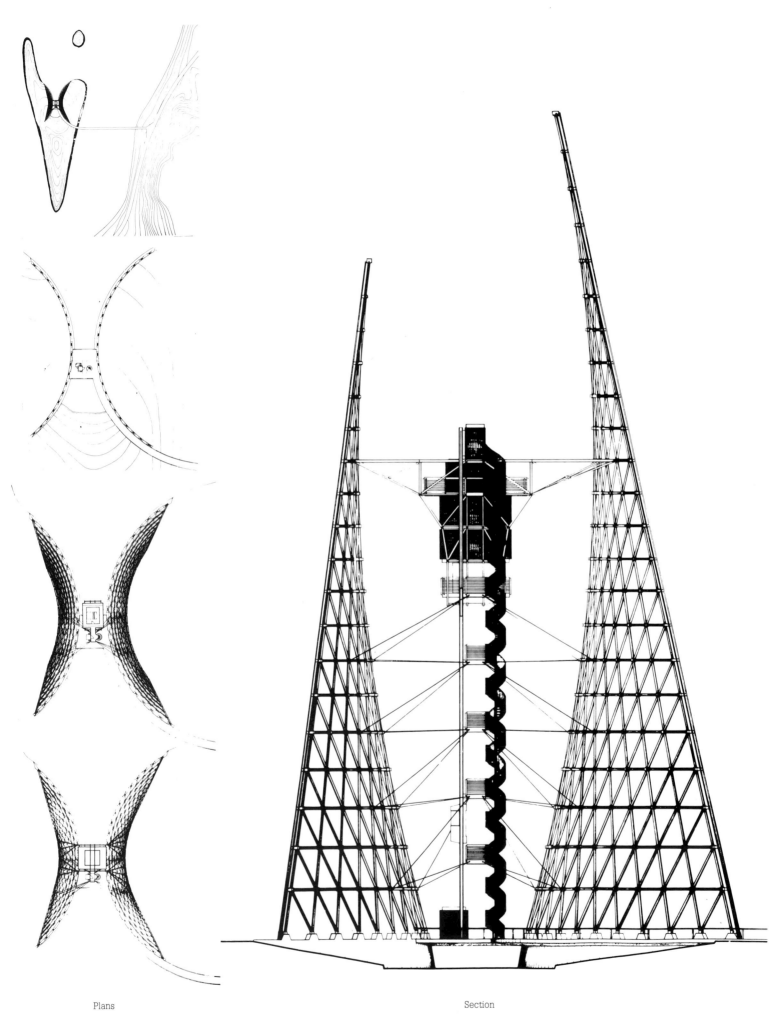

Plans

Section

Eastfield County Primary School
Leicestershire
previously named Thurmaston Junior School

1968

Leicestershire County Council's approach to education was forward looking and experimental. Our brief was a progression from earlier schools – the ideas extended and developed. We were asked to design a two-form entry, 360 place Junior School, to be built in two stages. Phase 1 consisted of four classrooms, multi-purpose hall, kitchen and administrative accommodation. A further two classrooms and the Library area were subsequently added.

The building is seen as a positive contribution to the development of specific educational aims and methods – a move away from the concept of the class as a self-contained unit, an encouragement of activities in varying sized units and a mixing of age groups. We were explicitly required to find a form which would encourage the use of the entire school by all children. Children are given a choice of activities. They are encouraged to use the Library – which is regarded as a central element in the plan – and not always to 'ask teacher'. An open plan was required, yet the importance of private corners was stressed.

A building was required 'in which the most up to date approaches to the education of children between the ages of 7 – 11 are possible', a building which is 'architecturally exciting and in keeping with the spirit of children of junior school age'.

The school is conceived as a compact complex of linked spaces, largely open plan and of varying scale ranging from small 'quiet rooms' to the main hall and designed to give the maximum variety and flexibility in use.

The teaching accommodation is in a large top-lit single storey area. The main entrance, using the slope of the site, is into the upper level of a 2-storey block, adjacent to the administrative accommodation, and leading to a focal point at which one descends half a level to the main floor. Two routes radiate from here at right angles, through the 'communal' spaces: hall, library and central court to the classroom areas. The classrooms are entirely open to a wide circulation route, which both links them together and forms an extension to the classroom area itself – the 'practical' area. Pairs of classrooms are further linked by a small 'resource' area which can be used as a small quiet room or can be opened to either one or both classrooms. There is a progression through large communal to small 'private' and 'child scale' spaces, getting away from the traditional concept of 'rooms' almost entirely.

Over 15 years after the school had opened, the headmaster wrote:

'This school has grown even more pleasant to work in over the years as we have lived in it and used it' . . . 'Visitors find it strikingly light, open and cheerful, and have difficulty in believing that it was opened as long ago as 1968.'

Client
Leicestershire County Council
Structural Engineer
Jenkins and Potter
M&E Engineer
Engineering Design Consultants
Quantity Surveyor
Gleeds
Area 1144 m²

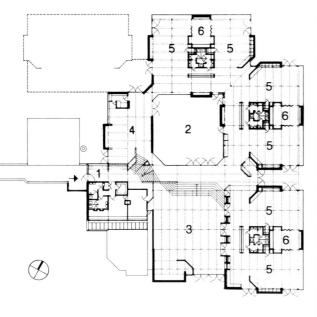

Ground floor plan

1 Main Entrance
2 Courtyard
3 Multi-purpose/Assembly Hall
4 Library
5 Classroom
6 Quiet Room

View from main entrance

Courtyard with 'Play Sculpture' by Norman Dilworth

Outdoor work area

Multi-purpose hall

Classroom

View towards main entrance from the multi-purpose hall with first floor staff area

St. Martin's Youth Project
St. Martin-in-the-Fields, London
1973

The Old National School building was designed by G.L. Taylor in 1830 on land immediately behind St. Martin-in-the-Fields. Our brief was to adapt the historic listed building for use as a Youth Centre and meeting place for young people, both visitors and Londoners.

The conversion was designed to exploit the natural variety of spaces and ceiling heights in the old structure and to restore the building to its inherent elegance and simplicity. A service alley behind the building was glazed over to provide extra space and became the main reception and information centre. The ground floor windows at the back of the building onto the alley way were opened up to give free access along the length of the interior into the major ground floor space which became the clubroom and bar which was fitted with semi-transparent screens and purpose-made furniture.
The old staircases were retained – one of them a splendid cast-iron structure at either end of the building linking the club room to the upper floors.

The first floor was converted into a large multi-purpose hall suitable for a variety of activities, performances, and meetings and the top floor with its smaller and lower rooms is used for a variety of individual and small group activities. There is also a warden's flat. The fine 1830 elevation to St. Martin's churchyard was restored and painted.

Client
The Centre at
St Martin-in-the-Fields

Structural Engineer
F.J. Samuely & Partners

Services Engineer
Max Fordham

Quantity Surveyor
D.A. Degerdon & Partners

General Contractor
P.G. Evans & Son

Area 805 m²

Main facade facing St. Martin-in-the-Fields after restoration

Main entrance in former rear alley

Bar and social area on the ground floor

Templeton College
Oxford

Oxford Centre for Management Studies

Phase 1: 1969-900 m²
Phase 2: 1974-900 m²
Phase 3: 1978-900 m²
Phase 4: 1979-484 m²

Phase 5: 1982-490 m²
Phase 6: 1987-920 m²
Phase 7: 1990-682 m²

In contrast to the 'one off' projects on which we have worked, this building is part of an indeterminate growth pattern. Our brief from the Oxford Centre for Management Studies as it was then named, was to allow for indefinite expansion. We attempted to find a pattern or framework based on a functional analysis of a complex problem. The building consists of three main components, each with different growth characteristics:

1. Study/bedrooms, repetitive, cellular growth.
2. Teaching rooms, a variety of spaces with uncertainty about future requirements and different types of teaching method.
3. Social and communal spaces, expansion of existing facilities, e.g. larger dining room, etc.

The overall pattern was devised to accommodate these different characteristics. It takes the form of a tartan grid superimposed diagonally on a main central spine forming the axis of growth. Teaching and communal spaces are on the spine, while the residential accommodation takes the form of a zigzag along the perimeter. Their overall order has responded well to a varied and rich brief over nearly 20 years.

Situated in Kennington to the south of Oxford, the site has a 1:15 gradient from southwest to northwest. The site is entered from the Kennington Road by way of the access road which leads the visitor obliquely to the building. From the Car Park the approach is continued up a stepped ramp to the Entrance Hall which forms the hub of the building from which major circulation routes emanate.

From the Entrance Hall, an enclosed bridge crosses the courtyard to connect with a high level walkway in the Residential Block, thus linking all three main areas by enclosed circulation routes. There is also ground level access through the courtyard.

The teaching area has been designed around a central, double volume toplit space, forming the Library or Information Centre. On the ground floor this is enclosed by Seminar and Teaching Rooms which have access to the Library. The upper level perimeter circulation routes form a gallery giving access to the Administrative Offices and other teaching rooms.

The communal area consists of Kitchen, Dining and Common Rooms linked public spaces in a single storey structure.

The residential area contains 53 study bedrooms in four groups. Because of the slope of the site and the dual purpose to which each room is put, the rooms themselves are split level spaces. One level is designed for living and studying, the other for sleeping.

Numerous craftsmen and artists have made contributions to create a fusion of art and architecture.

Since the first phase was completed in 1969, the college has been steadily expanding and a number of subsequent additions have been completed. Plans for further growth are now being considered.

Client
Templeton College
Quantity Surveyor
Phase 1
E. C. Harris & Partners
All other Phases
Northcroft, Neighbour
& Nicholson

Structural Engineer
F.J. Samuely & Partners
M & E Engineer
Phase 1
Engineering Design Consultants
All other Phases
James Briggs & Partners

Approach to main entrance

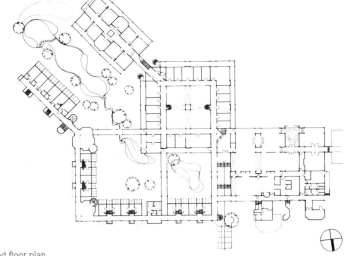

Ground floor plan

View from across the river

View from the meadows

Conference Room with table by Fred Baier

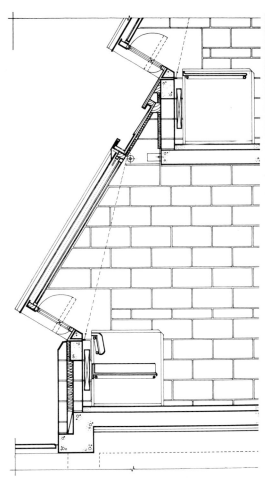

Detail of sloping glazing

Sloping glazing to study bedrooms

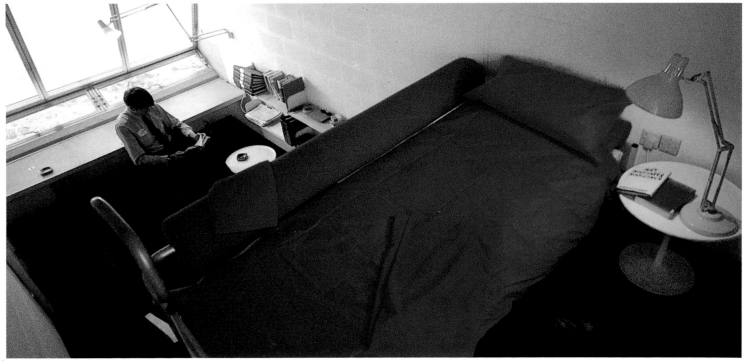

Study bedroom with lower working area

Information Centre

Detail of north elevation

Elevation of Dining Area and Common Room

Redcar District Library
Yorkshire

1971

The designs for new libraries at Redcar and Maidenhead are in many respects similar, taking the form of individual envelopes around similar design briefs. Their individuality is established by their siting, construction, form and materials. At Redcar, on heavy industrial Teeside, with its long association with the steel industry, it seemed appropriate to conceive a building that was essentially black and made of steel.

The brief was developed in consultation with the Department of Education and Science. Its primary objective is summarised in one of the Department's notes: 'The library should never be considered as a monument or as a cultural retreat; but as a source of pleasure, recreation, information and learning; readily available to all . . .'

The spirit of this idea is reflected in the careful siting of the building within a group of other social facilities, a deliberately uninstitutional character and an open, welcoming plan. Quiet areas are reserved on an upper level for reference, research and study. There is a specially designed area for children. A coffee bar and exhibition space are integrated in the design as part of the entrance to the building. Each section has been designed to be open and accessible to everyone.

The library facilities are planned for efficient organisation without sacrificing variety and interest in the lending area. The children's library is an informal design, including special mobile furniture, and planned round an internal court that can be used for story telling.

The structure consists of steel columns with long span castellated beams supporting a folded roof whose profile forms continuous rooflights over most of the floor area. The steel structure is in some cases extended in order to support the furniture which was also designed by the architects. The walls are of blue Staffordshire engineering bricks and of corrugated vinyl coated steel.

View towards main entrance

Client
Greater Teesdale Authority, formerly Redcar Urban District Council

Structural Engineer
F.J. Samuely & Partners

Services Engineer
Engineering Design Consultants

Quantity Surveyor
D.A. Degerdon & Partners

General Contractor
Laurence James Ltd

Area 2,000 m²

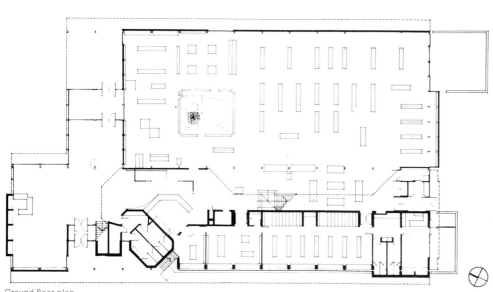

Ground floor plan

Main Library area

Main entrance and coffee area with covered link to Wintergarden

St. Andrew's College
Booterstown, Dublin

1968-1972

The decision to re-house the school in a new building and on a new site presented an opportunity and an obligation to re-examine its educational programme. The objective was to determine a form and organisation for the school which would accommodate present teaching methods but lean towards and encourage the rapid changes taking place in education.

St. Andrew's was a boys' school in the process of becoming co-educational. The brief required a secondary school for 300 pupils, a Junior School for 100 pupils and residential accommodation for 60 boarders and some staff. All parts of the school are planned together within a single structure to encourage a natural integration between Seniors and Juniors, day pupils and boarders.

To achieve this, two complementary ideas were explored: the first a method of zoning the principal functions within the school, the second a structural system which could provide a very fluid and responsive building form. Zoning was based on two parallel routes either side of a multi-purpose assembly hall at the heart of the building. All secondary day-school teaching is located in clusters on one side of the routes while on the other side are communal uses with residential accommodation above on an upper floor. At one end of the route is the Junior School, at the other, the sports facilities.

The assembly halls can be opened along both sides onto the routes to provide a generous open space at the centre of the building.

The structural idea developed into a system of bays which provide both a planning and a structural module. The primary structure consists of pre-cast reinforced concrete columns and beams with plywood cross-beams and roof panels capped with continuous rooflights. The roof structure also forms a distribution system for services which are readily accessible at any point.

Teaching takes place in a variety of spaces of different size and character, grouped according to subject around informal houserooms, each adjacent to a small garden court. The aim was to introduce in the teaching area a quality of liveliness and informality – a deliberate rejection of institutional character – and a further aid to the integration of activities and age groups.

Client
Board of Governors,
St. Andrew's College
Structural Engineer
Ove Arup & Partners, Dublin
Services Engineer
Varming Mulcahy Reilly
Associates
Quantity Surveyor
Patterson Kempster Shortall
General Contractor
John Sisk & Son Ltd.
Area 5,716 m²

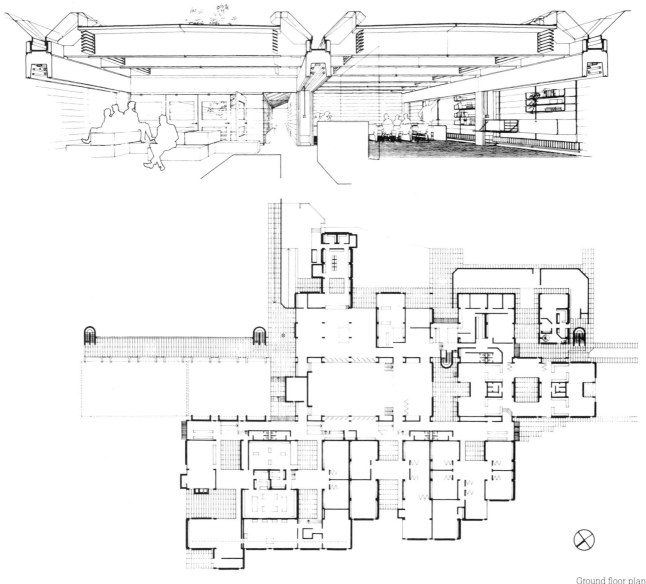

Ground floor plan

Typical classroom

Main Assembly Hall

Junior Assembly Hall

View from the playing fields

Reference Library

Entrance

Story-telling court outside children's library

Maidenhead Library
Berkshire
1972

The old library and war memorial garden at Maidenhead shared a site opposite the Town Hall dominated by a superb cedar tree. Behind the site, and at a lower level, access to the Central Bus Station was cut off by a small stream. A new building was required to provide an adequate library service for the town. As the existing library service had to be maintained during construction, it was decided to build the new library on the war memorial garden site and then to demolish the old library to provide a new public open space. By bridging the stream, a new and busy pedestrian route was created alongside the library linking the bus station to the heart of town. The great cedar tree became a pivot or hinge between the two sites.

A square plan on three levels was developed from the design brief which was essentially similar to that for the Redcar library. The building has many similar features. It was natural to plan the principal public facilities of the new building on the ground floor, with easy access and an open, welcoming atmosphere. Ground level therefore provided for the main lending library, children's library, music library and exhibition space. The main entrance faces onto the new route passing through the site across the stream. On an upper level, designed as part of the main volume but sufficiently separate for quiet and privacy, are reference and study sections and meeting rooms. Below, in a semi-basement taking advantage of the steep slope of the site down to the stream, are the bookstacks, administration and staff rooms and provision for a mobile library service.

The generous overhang of the roof, apparently floating over the enclosing glass wall and smaller brick structures, takes its inspiration from the cedar tree. It also, as at Redcar, gives the building an open, welcoming and anti-institutional character.

The building has two distinct scales: the large scale of the roof as a simple square plane sheltering and giving unity to the whole volume below, and a small-scale village of varied spaces created by the brick structures below.

The roof is a clear-span space-frame which was constructed on the ground and jacked up into position where it is supported independently from the rest of the structure by eight cruciform reinforced concrete columns. A secondary structure supports the mezzanine gallery inside. Large bay window elements, their tops splayed at the same angle as the space-frame overhang above, contribute to the profile of the interior space by providing protected alcoves for a variety of functions and are also principal modulating elements on the exterior.

Client
Maidenhead Borough Council
General Contractor
Walden & Son
Quantity Surveyor
D.A. Degerdon & Partners
Services Engineer
Engineering Design Consultants
Structural Engineer
F.J. Samuely & Partners
Area 1,988 m²

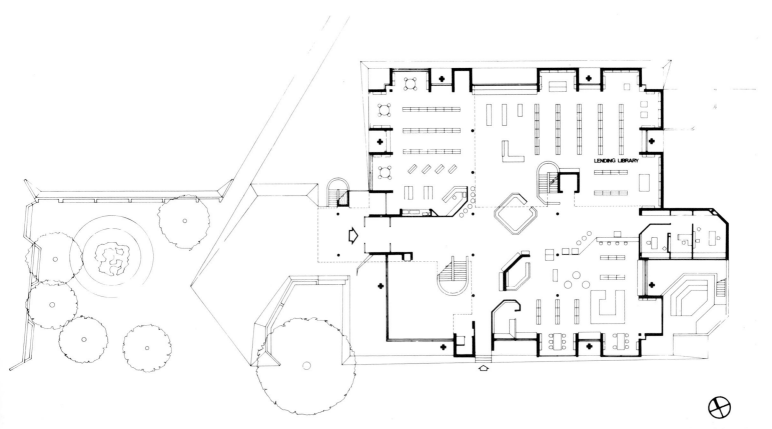

Ground floor plan

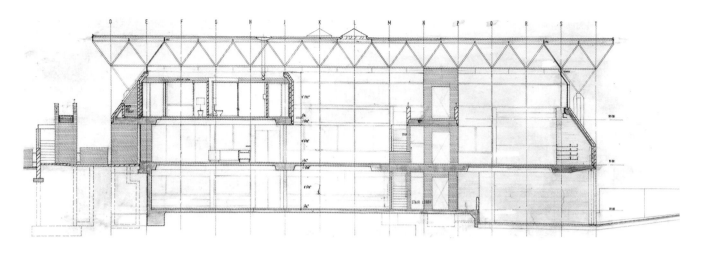

Section

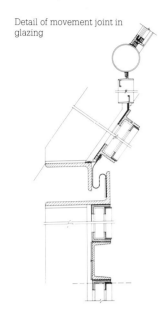
Detail of movement joint in glazing

Detail of space frame

Erection of space frame roof structure

Exhibitions at New London Gallery
London

1961 and 1963 Henry Moore 1963 Ben Nicholson

The exhibition of Henry Moore's pre-war sculpture at the New
London Gallery required a display that would reveal the
individual character of each work and yet provide a context
which would define a character of its own without dominating
or detracting from the superb quality of the sculpture. The
pieces were carefully considered, individually and in groups,
for scale, contrast and appropriate lighting so that their sheer
quantity in the small space would not be too apparent and so
that it would be possible to enjoy each work in its own right
as well as the collection as a whole.

The exhibition of Ben Nicholson's paintings and reliefs in the
same gallery displayed his work on structures and surfaces
whose profiles and forms were designed to echo and
complement the character of the artist's work.

Client
Marlborough Fine Art Ltd

Henry Moore Exhibition 1961

Ben Nicholson Exhibition 1963

Chalvedon Housing
Basildon New Town

1968

Phase 1: 1975 Area 1 425 housing units
Phase 2: 1976 Area 2 371 housing units
Phase 3: 1977 Area 3 583 housing units

The brief was to design 1,400 homes for 5,000 people on 33 hectares of land in the east of Basildon New Town.

The design strategy sought to organise the very large number of homes into smaller groupings which would be both more manageable and more comprehensible to the people living there by identifying each group with a particular space on the site. This was to be done in a manner that would achieve pedestrian and vehicular segregation without placing unnecessary or artificial restrictions on people's mobility.

Groups of 60 one- and two-storey houses, each with its own private garden, enclose large communal gardens which are completely traffic-free and safe for small children. Local traffic enters the site on a cul-de-sac system to discourage through traffic but provides for essential short journeys, particularly to the small commercial and social centre, without affecting the major town roads.

The groups of houses sharing their larger communal gardens are all built of simple materials – brick, concrete tiles and stained timber – but each group varies in size, shape and character to give a variety of spaces and routes throughout the site. The scheme includes a small centre incorporating social and community facilities and a few shops.

The houses themselves are designed with potential for variation of internal planning. The family houses each have two living rooms – one of which can be used as a dining room or as a combined family room. Double bedrooms can be divided into two single rooms; single bedrooms can double as studies or small dining rooms.

It was interesting to discover that the single storey house types had far greater inherent flexibility when it came to providing a choice to the user, and they were also much more responsive to family living, growth and change than the more traditional two-storey house where problems of frontage and layout made such adaptability much more difficult. They also suited old and disabled people.

A great deal of social research was carried out to inform the brief for the later stages of the project and particularly the Centre. Contacts were established with the local community foreshadowing the techniques of 'community architecture'.

Client
Basildon Development
Corporation
Structural Engineer
F.J. Samuely & Partners
Services Engineer
R.M. Wilson
Quantity Surveyor
E.C. Harris & Partners
General Contractor
C.S. Wiggins & Sons Ltd.

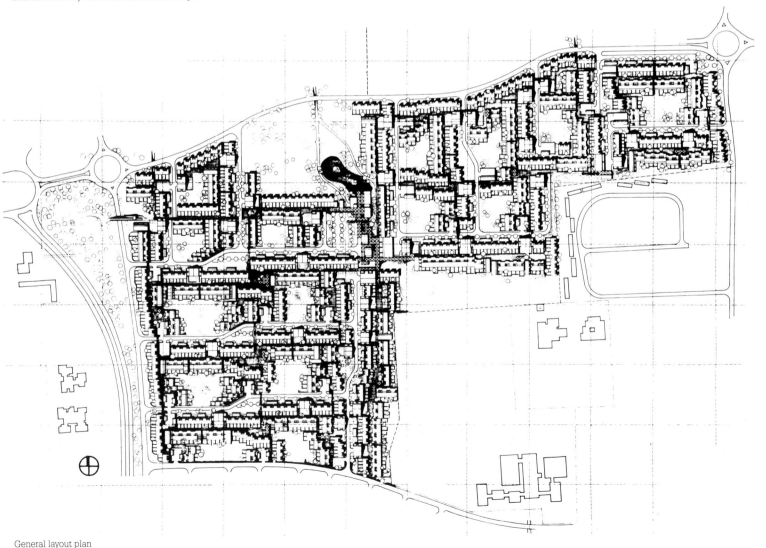

General layout plan

Single storey houses

Garden side to houses

A group of houses for the elderly close to family homes

Community Hall

Living room in single storey house

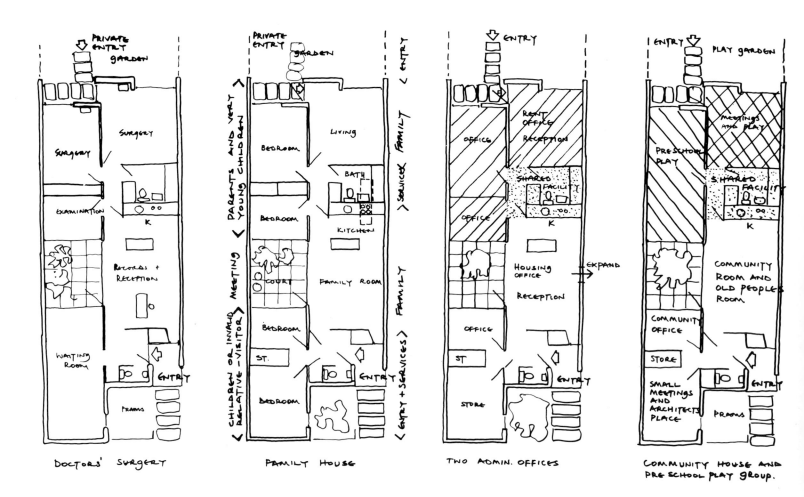

DOCTORS' SURGERY

FAMILY HOUSE

TWO ADMIN. OFFICES

COMMUNITY HOUSE AND PRE SCHOOL PLAY GROUP.

Chalvedon Housing. Six person single storey house indicating different uses

Basildon S.W. Area Study

1968

This was a planning study for a major extension to Basildon, undertaken in association with the Development Corporation, to provide for an additional population of 20,000 people in an area of outstanding natural beauty to the south-west of Basildon New Town.

The quality of the landscape encouraged the idea of neighbourhood zones to create the closest possible relationship between housing and open countryside without sacrificing ease of access to the town centre.

Traffic growth in the town and surrounding region required a major new road from the south-eastern to the north-western ends of the site to provide direct access to the town centre. This road was aligned with the existing railway to allow the new neighbourhood villages to extend as individual spurs into the surrounding countryside.

Each spur was planned for a population of about 5,000 people – large enough to support primary education but small enough for all children to be able to walk to school.

This pattern established four independent spurs of housing separated by generous fringes of natural landscape which penetrate as far as the existing edge of the town. Each neighbourhood spur is based on a spine road branching from the new major town connector road into the countryside, with banks of housing on either side served by a series of branch roads. At the heart of each spur there is a primary school and a small local centre providing for daily shopping, welfare, social and employment needs. A footpath system, parallel to the spine road, connects the individual housing groups by a system of underpasses.

The study was intended to establish planning guidelines and principles which would give form and coherence to the housing groups, which would subsequently be designed by various architects.

Client
Basildon Development
Corporation
Structural Engineer
F.J. Samuely & Partners
Quantity Surveyor
E.C. Harris & Partners

Microclimatologist
Professor E.T. Stringer
Geologist
J.N. Hutchinson
Traffic Engineer
The Chief Engineer, Basildon
Development Corporation

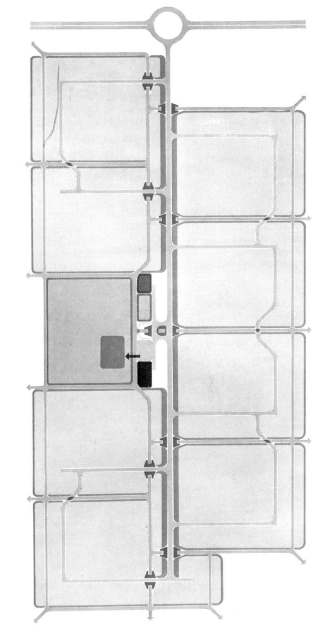

Theoretical spur diagram

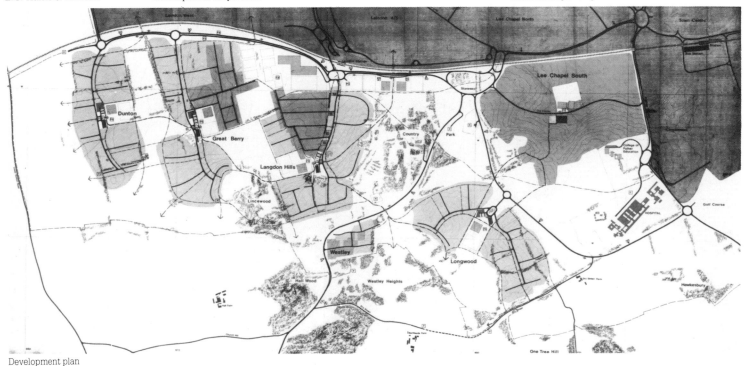

Development plan

Nebenzahl House
Jerusalem
1968-1972

The site in the Jewish Quarter of the Old City of Jerusalem, just inside the Old City Wall, overlooks the Western Wall, the Temple Mount and Dome of the Rock with magnificent views ranging from Mount Zion and the Valley of Kidron, to the Mount of Olives and Mount Scopus, to the hills of the Judean Desert in the far distance.

Our client required three separate apartments, each on a single level, with a common entrance court and a guest flat at ground level. Views from the building and its location played an extremely important part in the brief, not only for their scenic value but also because of their powerful religious and emotional content and associations. Legislation required that all external surfaces – including walls, roofs and pavings – be of stone.

The house was designed to blend unobtrusively into the Old City without resorting to a pastiche of the traditional buildings but achieving a sense of quality with simplicity and without ostentation or pretension.

The house continues the existing line of buildings which follow the line of the City Wall and which step with it down the hill. Its form and scale are carefully related to these and other surrounding buildings and the stonework pays careful attention to the spirit of traditional masonry.

The outer enclosing wall is penetrated by openings designed to reveal the many different views that the site commands, not all at once, but by subtle degrees through deep window reveals which filter and reflect the magical and ever-changing light that is unique to Jerusalem.

Client
Dr. I.E. Nebenzahl
Consultant Architect
Joseph Schoenberger,
Jerusalem
Supervising Architect
Reuven Druckman, Jerusalem
Structural Engineer
J. Kahan & Lev, Jerusalem
Services Engineer
J. Ascher, Jerusalem
Quantity Surveyor
J. Kahan and Lev, in assoc.
with Monk Dunstone, London
General Contractor
Benyav, Jerusalem
Area 1,200 m^2

View towards the Dome of the Rock

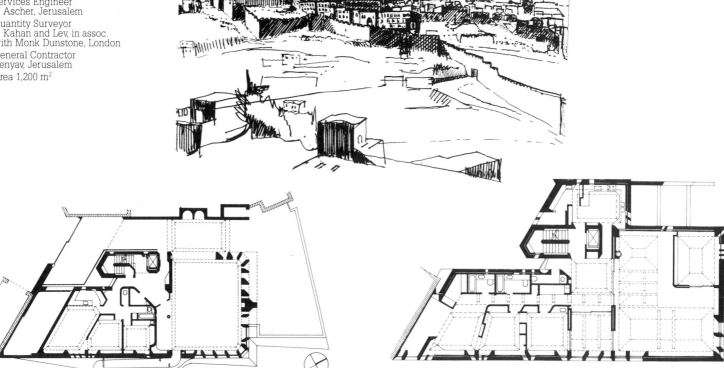

Ground floor plan

Plan of third floor apartment

Construction photographs

View from entrance court towards the Dome of the Rock

View over the Old City Wall

Living room of the principal apartment

77

Keble College
Oxford

Phase 1: 1972
Phase 2: 1976
Phase 3: 1980

These residential rooms for Keble College Oxford were designed to be constructed in two phases on an extremely constricted site, with the implicit understanding that the new building would co-exist sympathetically with the extraordinary High-Church-Anglican-Gothic inventions of William Butterfield, built a century ago. The third phase consisted of various alterations to the existing building.

The new building was conceived as a 'wall', one room thick, each room having a two-way aspect for both view and ventilation, the wall coiling around the southern end of the site to enclose a new small quadrangle. An austere exterior perimeter of brick, punctuated by vertical service towers and slot windows, emphasised the 'wall' idea, while on the inside of its protective shell is a soft underbelly of glass formed of overlapping planes which descend to shelter a continuous walkway. The uncoiled spiral plan became the pattern of movement, a building form containing the seeds of growth, which capitalises on the restricted space, and creates a major new space for the College.

The walkway leads to staircases giving access to pairs of rooms on either side with services at each half landing, eliminating corridors and enabling the individual rooms to be as spacious as possible.

The third phase consisted of alterations and extensions to the Library and to the Bursary and administrative offices. The detailing of these, which included the furniture, takes its cue from the Gothic architecture without becoming merely imitative – a sympathetic new insertion.

Awards
1978 RIBA Award Southern Region
1981 Carpenters Award Phase 3

Client
Keble College Oxford
Structural Engineer
Ove Arup & Partners
Services Engineer
Zisman Bowyer & Partners
Quantity Surveyor
Northcroft Neighbour & Nicholson
General Contractor
Phase 1
Johnson & Bailey Ltd.
Phase 2
Benfield & Loxley Ltd.
Phase 3
Kingerlee Ltd.

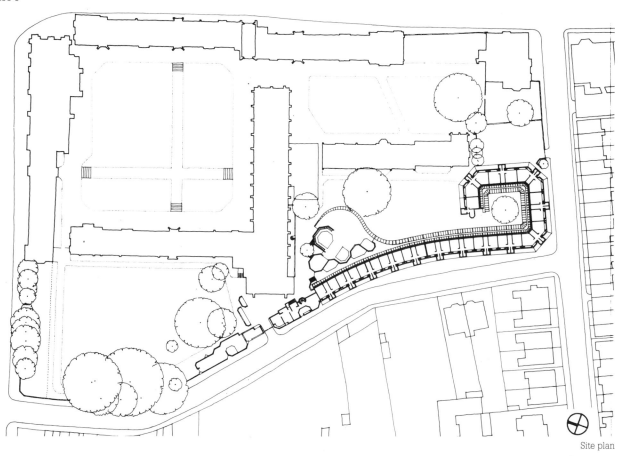

Site plan

Hayward Quad

The college bar

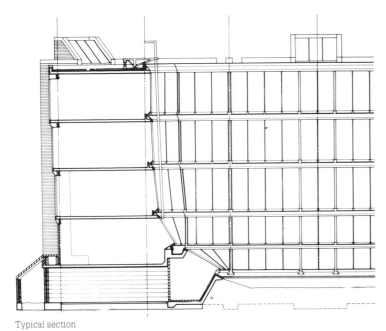

Typical section

Section through glazed access route

Bar at end of the glazed route   Typical study bedroom

The Library

The Bursary

Detail of Bursary furniture

Detail of Library stair

Post Office Headquarters Redevelopment

St. Martin's-le-Grand, London

Project

1975

The project for the headquarters of the Post Office Corporation was designed for an island site north of Newgate Street near St. Paul's Cathedral. The brief required maximum office use at a four-to-one plot ratio and the planning authority stipulated a maximum height of about 30 metres to protect distant views of the dome of St. Paul's.

From a series of site studies, the plan developed in the form of two large segments whose perimeter walls extended out to the irregularly shaped site boundaries. The segments were joined by a core of lifts and services and were offset on plan to form two new landscaped plazas in the south west and north east corners of the site. Pedestrians would circulate freely across the site through the centre of the building between the two plazas. Pedestrian bridges connected with the Paternoster Development to the south, the Greyfriars Christchurch Gardens to the west, and the existing Postal Headquarters building to the north.

In the southern segment there were seven floors of offices above an operationally independent Telex Switching Centre. In the northern segment there were five floors of offices above an amenities floor. The two top floors in both segments contained cellular offices planned around planted covered courtyards, the remaining levels being designed as deep plan landscaped offices.

The building was fully glazed, not as a hard brittle wall, but a deep tracery of bright metal superimposed as a lattice on the outer face of the glass. The overall effect of this lattice was to give the impression of a thick wall construction but with delicate and intricate detail when seen face-on.

The lattice supported the glazing and the window-cleaning gear and housed guides for automatically controlled semi-transparent blinds which were to be mounted on its outer face. Air conditioning energy was to be conserved by avoiding excessive heat gain through the glass, heat recovery and making maximum use of natural light around the perimeter of the building. The design developed from the irregular and curving forms of the site and exploited the unequal heights and volumes of the two major segments connected by pronounced vertical circulation towers. The combined effect of metal lattice, glass, blinds and curved surfaces created an external surface with an apparently ever-changing depth and varying pattern as the external blinds responded to changes of weather and season.

Client
Property Services Agency

Structural Engineer
Ove Arup & Partners

Services Engineer
H.L. Dawson & Associates

Quantity Surveyor
Monk Dunstone Mahon & Scears

Area 45,750 m^2

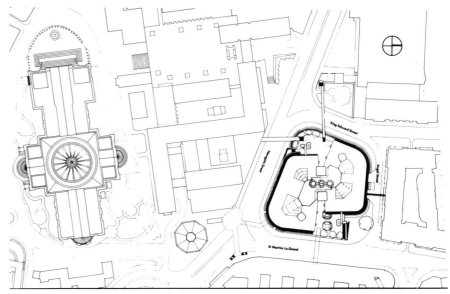

Location plan

Upper floor plan

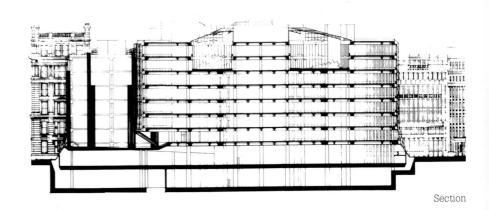

Section

84

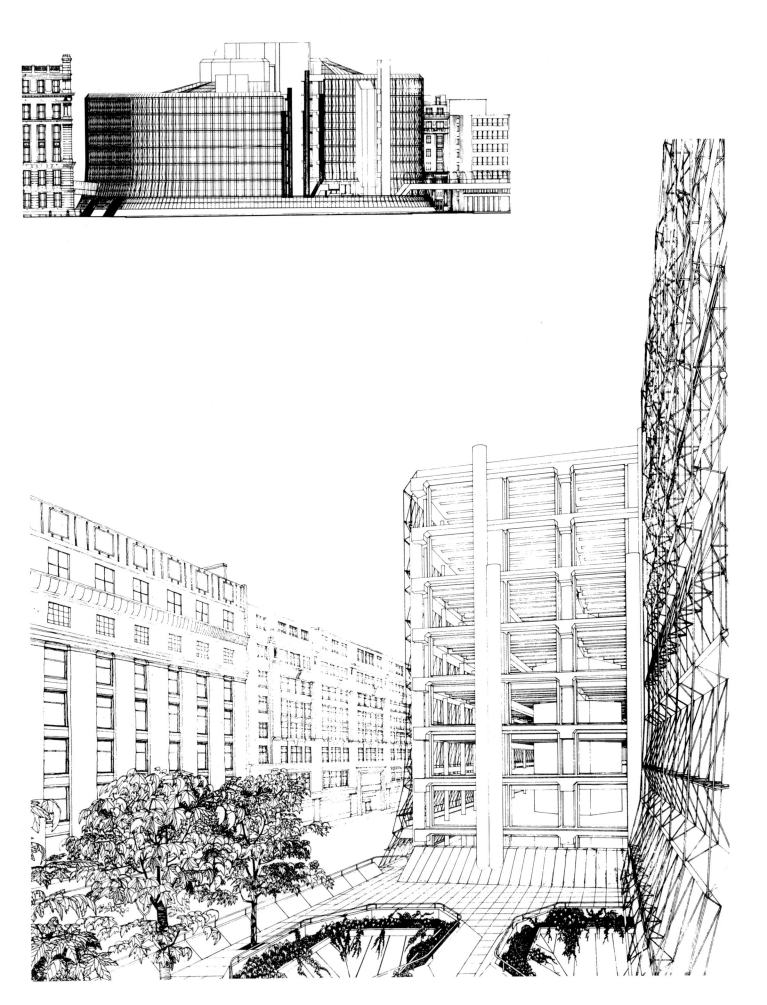

Post Office Headquarters model

Trinity College Arts Faculty Building
Dublin

1968-1979

The new Arts Building is conceived within the context of an expanding university structure and as a part of Trinity College as a whole. It is sited in the Old Fellows' Garden adjoining Nassau Street to the south. Together with the Old Library (Thomas Burgh 1732) and our Berkeley Library, the Arts Building encloses the new Fellows' Square. A new entrance to the College is formed from Nassau Street through the new building and Fellows' Square. The square contains a magnificent Alexander Calder stabile through the gift of a former student.

Our brief posed the problem of increasing the volume and density of the College buildings whilst maintaining, so far as possible, its present scale and character. We have tried to establish a hierarchy of spaces corresponding both to the whole organisation and to its component parts, to give a sense of the whole and yet at the same time to create variety and a sense of individuality and intimacy for the people using the building. Our proposal results in an unusually compact, deep plan building with its height restricted to below that of the Old Library opposite.

The building provides teaching facilities for over 200 Academic Staff and 3,700 graduates and undergraduates, incorporating the Faculties of Arts Humanities, Arts Letters, Economics and Social Studies.

The accommodation is divided into two main categories and is planned on five floors. The lower two levels contain the first category of non-departmental elements and include the principal Lecture Theatres including the 400 seat Edmund Burke Hall, the Lecky Library, the Faculty Administration, and the Douglas Hyde Gallery which is administered by the College jointly with the Irish Arts Council, all conceived around a single main concourse. This concourse forms a linear circulation spine to the building and acts as a focal element, with a small coffee shop, providing a social communal centre which has become the principal meeting and gathering place within the College. The concourse contains an outstanding collection of Modern Irish Painting obtained from the Irish Arts Council. The departmental accommodation is situated on the upper three floors and includes staff rooms and offices as well as smaller lecture and seminar rooms. These are organised as clusters of accommodation arranged in large areas of flexible floor space. The deep plan floors are penetrated by internal courts and indents and are stepped in section, each floor being cut back from that below, to allow light and air to penetrate to the central areas.

Client
Trinity College,
University of Dublin
Structural Engineer
Ove Arup & Partners
Services Engineer
Varming Mulcahy Reilly
Associates

Quantity Surveyor
Patterson Kempster &
Shortall
General Contractor
John Sisk & Son Ltd.
Area 16,700 m²

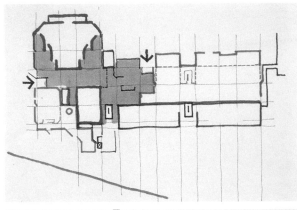

Lower concourse with lecture theatre

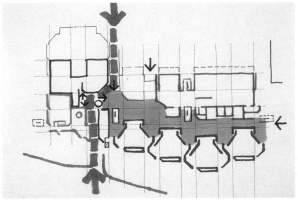

Upper concourse showing route through the building from the Nassau Street entrance to Fellows' Square

Entrance from Nassau Street

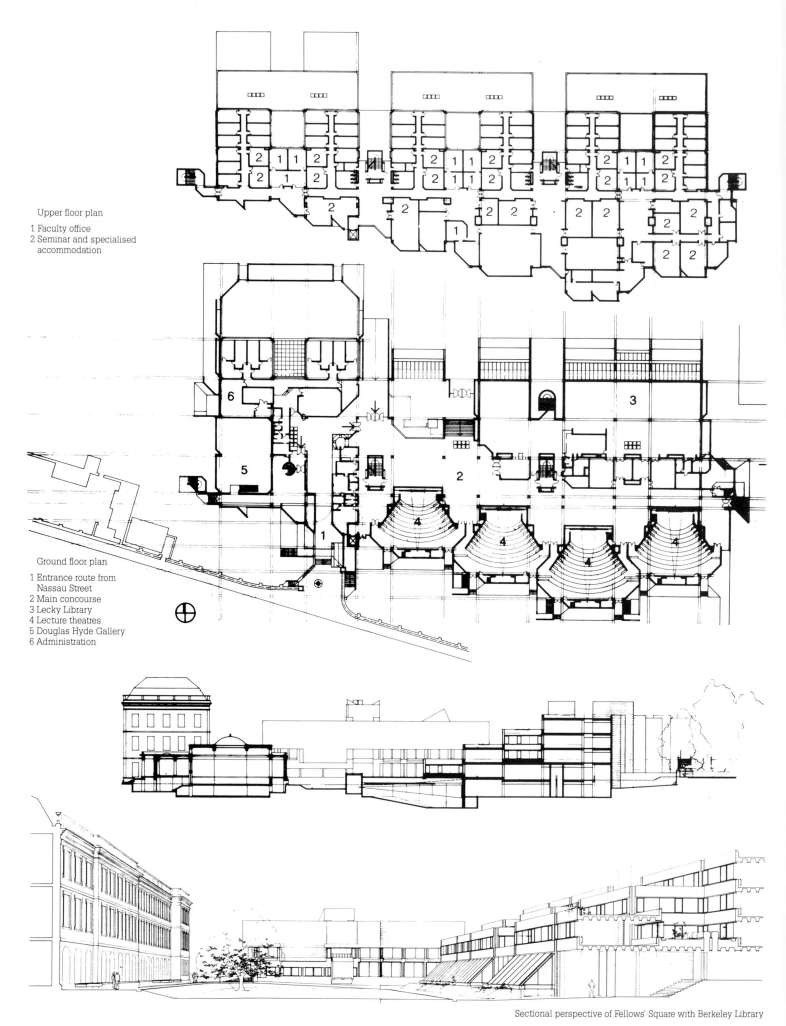

Upper floor plan

1 Faculty office
2 Seminar and specialised
  accommodation

Ground floor plan

1 Entrance route from
  Nassau Street
2 Main concourse
3 Lecky Library
4 Lecture theatres
5 Douglas Hyde Gallery
6 Administration

Sectional perspective of Fellows' Square with Berkeley Library

View across Fellows' Square from
Berkeley Library towards the
Provost's House

Berkeley Library seen from the
main entrance

Main entrance seen from Front Square

Main concourse

Lecky Library stairs

Antiquities Museum

Lecky Library reading area

Douglas Hyde Gallery

Two views of the
Edmund Burke Theatre
400-seat Lecture Theatre

Upper level concourse

Alexander Calder 'Stabile' in
Fellows' Square

East elevation from College Park

Plan Guinet, Valescure
Var, France

Project

1973

A development plan for a 240 Hectare site owned by Southern Real Estate Associates outside St Raphael in the South of France. A beautiful and hilly site, densely wooded with umbrella pines and ferns, and with extensive views to the sea, a few kilometres to the south, and to the mountains in the north. The development was to consist of a Championship Golf Course surrounded by housing with a luxury Hotel, Golf Club and auxillary commercial and sports facilities.

The housing was grouped in strategically placed clusters like small villages or hamlets around the golf course which formed the central feature of the scheme.

Client
Southern Real Estate
Associates
Structural Engineer
Ove Arup & Partners
Service Engineer
Ove Arup & Partners
Quantity Surveyor
Gardiner & Theobald

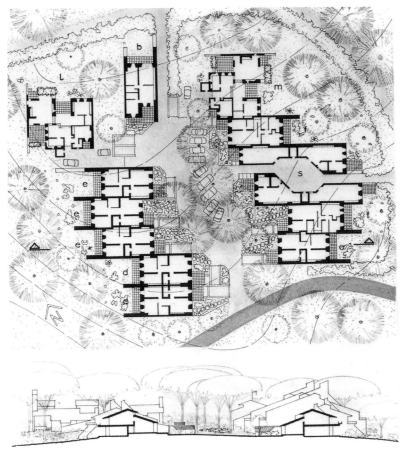

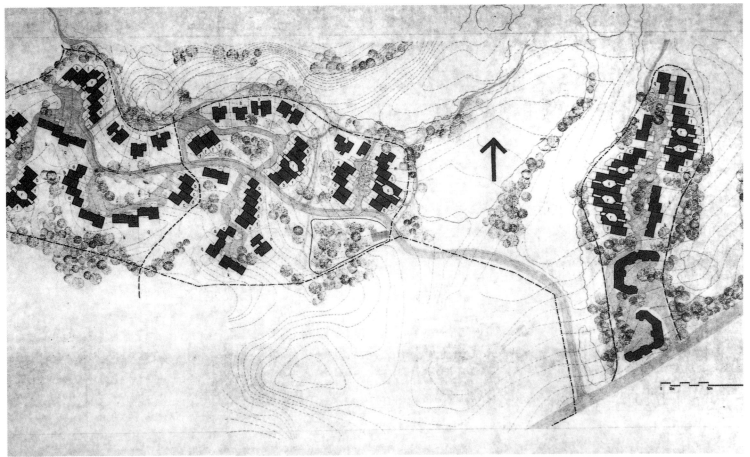

Typical housing cluster

General layout plan

Whitmore Court Housing
Basildon New Town

1975

This scheme for the Basildon Development Corporation provides 90 dwellings with walk up access, mainly for 1,2 and 3 persons at an over-all density of 78 people per acre. The client's intention was to provide homes for young single people and also to respond to the demand for old people's dwellings. One third of the total accommodation was designed specifically for old people. This mix of young and old was carefully considered at planning stage. A small Day Centre for old people was also provided. There are 20 garages and a further 62 parking places.

The site has a gentle fall from west to east and the flats are arranged in five blocks so that they enclose three warm and sunny open spaces protected from wind and noise. Several well established trees have been retained and they serve to define and give individuality to these spaces. The flats for old people are at ground and first floor level and are close to the Day Centre and to the Warden's Flat. Paths at various levels give access and the blocks are linked at their junctions. Access for vehicles is to the north and parking, deliveries and refuse collection points are within a short distance.

Construction is of light brown facing brick with pre-cast concrete facings to the planting boxes, and stained timber for the window frames.

Award
Good Design in Housing 1977

Client
Basildon Development Corporation
Structural Engineer
Charles Weiss & Partners
Services Engineer
Dale & Ewbank
Quantity Surveyor
E.C. Harris and Partners
General Contractor
Globe Construction Company Ltd.
Housing Units 90

Typical floor plan

1 Centre for the Elderly
2 Flats with one bedroom suitable for the elderly
3 Single person flats
4 Caretaker

94

Detail of elderly people's window boxes

Single people's accommodation

Habitat
Wallingford
1972-1974

Habitat required warehousing, offices and a showroom on a flat 4 acre site of rather indifferent industrial character on the outskirts of Wallingford. Implicit in the brief was the assumption that the new building should reflect and enhance Habitat's reputation for design.

With the warehouse building nearly ten times the volume of the showroom, the difference of scale was resolved by designing two similar structures like parent and child, distinguished not only by size but by a vivid contrast of colour: an acid green for the warehouse and cool white for the showroom.

The clear-span roof construction houses all services within the depth of the space frame and permits completely free planning of the layout of the warehouse and showroom area below.

In anticipation of people travelling quite far to buy household goods and furniture, the showroom has been designed to provide a day out for the family. There is ample car parking, a protected playground for small children, with play sculpture by Eduardo Paolozzi, which can be seen from within the showroom, and a small cafe-restaurant with an outside terrace. The white showroom stands on a raised podium of dark brick which also forms the connecting link between the two structures.

Awards
1976 Structural Steel Design Award
1976 Financial Times Industrial Architecture Award

Client	General Contractor
Habitat Designs Ltd	Myton Ltd
Structural Engineer	Interior Designer
Ove Arup & Partners	Conran Associates
Services Engineer	Area 7,645 m²
Ove Arup & Partners	
Quantity Surveyor	
Monk & Dunstone	

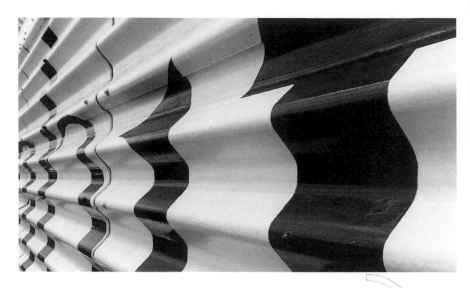

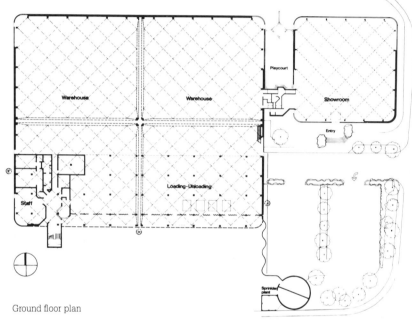

Ground floor plan

View of entrance

Showroom

Ground floor reading area

Phase 1 plant room

Night view towards Portsmouth Harbour

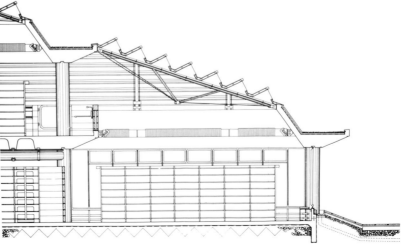

Section showing roof truss

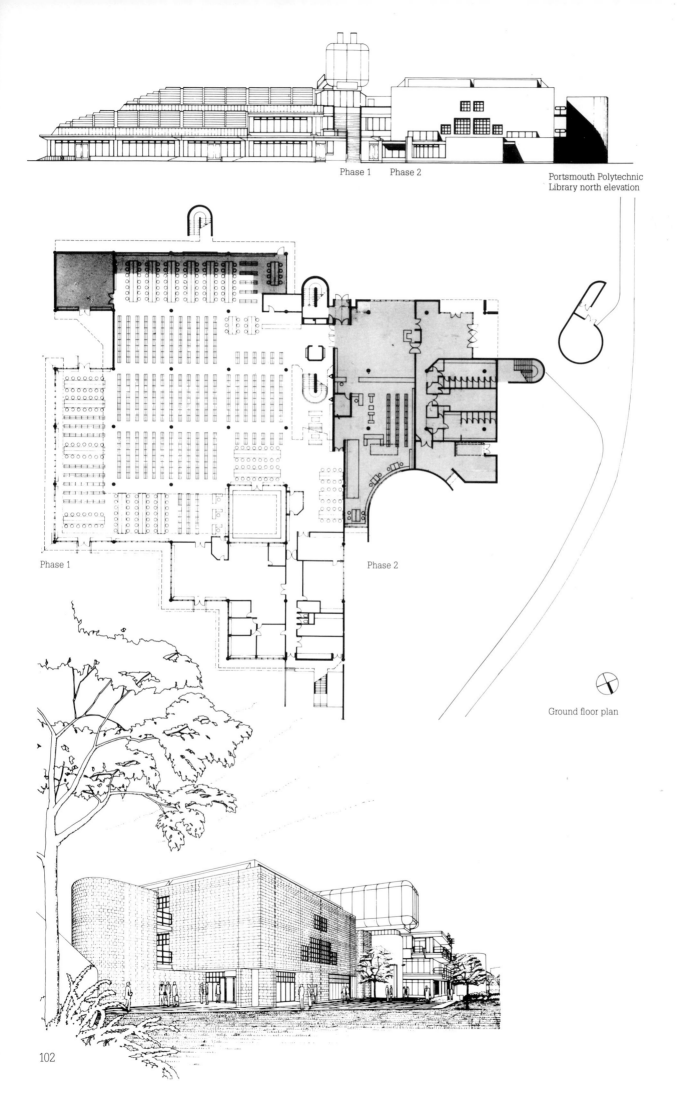

Phase 1　　　Phase 2

Portsmouth Polytechnic
Library north elevation

Phase 1

Phase 2

Ground floor plan

Felmore Housing
Basildon New Town

1974-1980

Following a planning study for 3,000 dwellings in the Northlands/Felmore area, we were commissioned to design 418 houses to current cost yardstick standards, as the first phase of the development.

This scheme is the first major housing project in the U.K. to use a number of techniques of energy conservation and particularly the principle of passive solar gain. The application of this principle, together with higher standards of insulation, draught-proofing and supervision ensured that a reduction of 30%-40% in energy use was achieved without sacrificing the quality and character of the built environment; on the contrary, energy considerations have reinforced the richness and variety of the scheme.

The houses are organised in three major identifiable groups separated by wide greens. Children's play areas are planned so as to minimise disturbance to the surrounding houses. The open spaces are planted with generous wind shelter belts.

The houses, which are one and two storeys high, all face south or near south. They are built of brick and timber incorporating high standards of insulation and carefully considered natural ventilation systems. The planning has been devised to give the tenants flexibility and choice in the way they live and all houses have dual access and gardens.

The major challenge at Felmore 1 was to create a socially and aesthetically successful community within the discipline given by energy conservation techniques and the constraints of low-cost housing budgets.

Client
Basildon Development Corporation
Structural Engineer
Ove Arup & Partners
Services Engineer
Ove Arup & Partners
Energy Consultant
George Kasabov
Quantity Surveyor
E.C. Harris & Partners
General Contractor
Phase 1:
Coward (Contractors) Ltd.
Phase 2:
C.S. Wiggins & Sons Ltd.
Housing Units 418

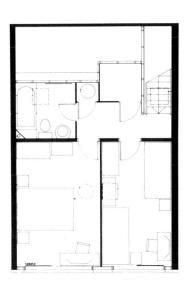

Ground floor plan two storey house   Upper floor plan

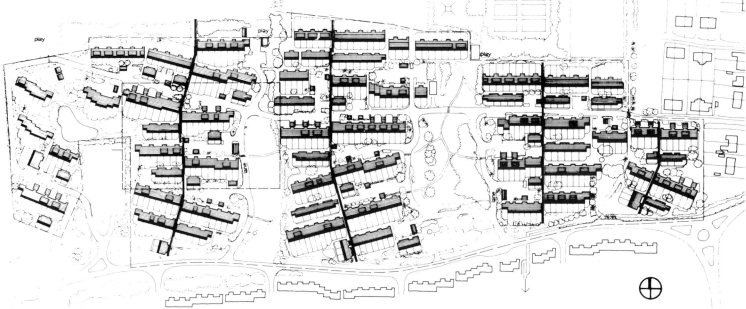

General layout plan

Sunlit spaces between houses

Single storey for the elderly near to family house

Houses with a southern orientation

Children's play spaces

The Covered Pedestrian Way

General view

Elevation of machining area

Machining area at night

Interior of machining area

House In Wicklow
Co. Wicklow, Eire

1979-1982

This house is built on a beautiful and remote site in Glencree high in the Wicklow mountains south of Dublin.

Although only 20 miles from the centre of Dublin, it is still largely unspoilt mountain scenery. The aim of the design is to insert the house unobtrusively into the landscape whilst shaping the house to take full advantage of the varied views from the site.

The site slopes steeply up to the north and the house is cut in to the hillside. The plan is in the form of an L-shape around a large central hall which is a glass-roofed double height volume linking the main part of the house to a guest flat and additional bedroom at the upper level. All the principal rooms face south east and south west. The living area consisting of living room, dining room and kitchen, faces the long view down the valley to the south east. The main bedroom is at a slightly lower level and faces into a small glade in the bottom of the valley within sight and sound of the stream.

The construction is of reinforced concrete, roofs planted with grass and heather, external walls in rubble masonry of local granite. The house is largely glazed to the south with sliding timber screens and panels.

Services Consultant
Varming Mulcahy Reilly
Quantity Surveyor
Patterson Kempster & Shortall
Approximate gross area 400 m^2

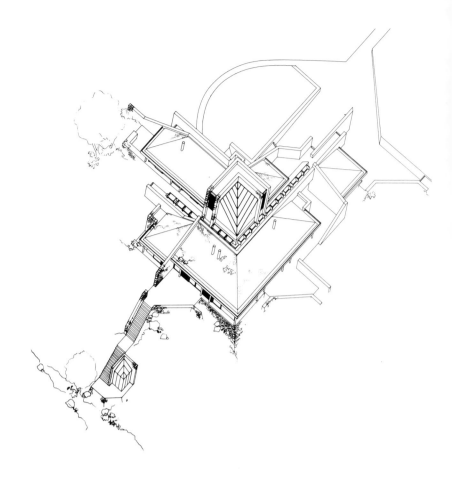

View of central hall from top of stair

Approach to the main entrance

Southwest elevation of living room

British Airports Authority
Gatwick Airport

Project for Head Office

1977

This Preliminary Study looked beyond conventional solutions towards a new interpretation of the office function. The problem was seen in terms of a need to reconcile the requirements of the organisation as a whole and those of the individual within it. On the one hand, the need of the organisation for a sense of unity, communication and flexibility in response to growth and change and on the other hand, the need of the individual for a sense of identity and location and a variable degree of privacy.

It had also become necessary to develop fundamentally new attitudes to the use of energy in buildings and to provide an appropriate and comfortable environment in both physical and psychological terms whilst minimizing the cost, particularly in relation to energy use and maintenance.

The elimination of aircraft noise was the overriding consideration on this site. This resulted in a sealed building with artificial ventilation which in turn required air conditioning. It is possible to provide this without the high energy use normally entailed. The design aimed at achieving a reduction of between 50% and 60% of the energy used in a conventional building of this type.

A very low building was proposed, largely on two floors which incorporate all the office accommodation, two thirds of the office area being on the lower or ground floor with one third on the first floor and the catering and recreation complex on a third upper level.

Client
British Airports
Authority
Structural &
Environmental Engineer
Ove Arup & Partners
Acoustics Consultants
Kenneth Shearer & Associates
Area 14,500 m^2

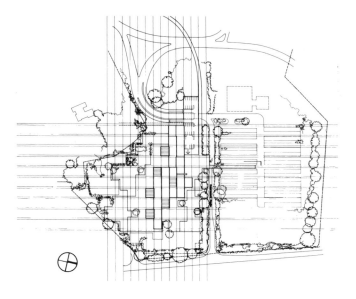

Ground floor plan

View of model

Sketch of main entrance

Johnson and Johnson Head Office
Slough

Project

1978

The design and quality of the building aims to reflect Johnson and Johnson's 'dominant international position in the research, manufacture and marketing of high quality health care products.'

The form of our proposal reflects Johnson and Johnson's tradition of 'small is beautiful' and embodies and encourages a sense of the identity and autonomy of divisions within the context of an integrated organisation. This requires a real sense of identity and quality beyond the gloss or glamour of a smart modern office interior as well as a recognition that the building is in fact a workshop – or tool for those who use it.

Our design aims to reflect Johnson and Johnson's care for its customers, products and staff. The building opens itself to the world at its entrance so that the relationship of Johnson and Johnson to their customers is demonstrated. We have consciously avoided the impression of a 'fortress' or a building which rejects outsiders. The informal and articulated shape of the building and the breakdown in scale creates this impression and planting also helps in this as the intermediary between insider and outsider.

The design sets out to be beautiful yet functional, efficient yet human, innovatory yet relevant, of great quality but not overtly extravagant.

This office building broke the tradition of 'services in the ceiling' and was one of the first designs to propose an overall computer floor. The use of passive cooling was integrated into an overall idea for energy conservation.

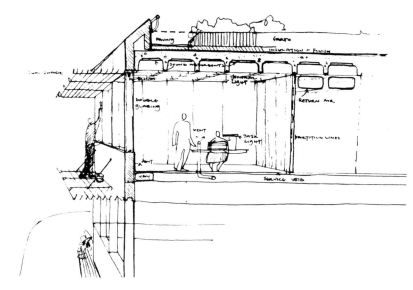

Sketch section showing structure and environmental control systems

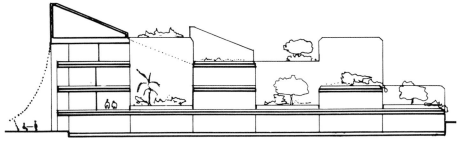

Typical section

Client
Johnson and Johnson
Structural & Environmental
Engineers
Ove Arup & Partners

Planning Consultant
Frank Duffy
Area 103,000 m²

View of model

Callands Action Area Plan
Warrington New Town

Project

1980

A scheme for the development of about 96 Hectares for housing and associated facilities and for a public open space, consisting of Callands Fields in the centre, including the two major existing woodlands and Sankey Valley Linear Park along the eastern boundary. The area will accommodate about 5,600 people.

The concept takes the form of a 'village' around Callands Fields with a comprehensible and ordered plan and yet with a potential for great variety. The plan capitalises on the existing natural features by complementing and developing them. A varied street character is proposed intensifying at the Local Centre (initially 2-3 shops and a Public House but with potential for other uses by possible conversion of ground floor flats).

The Callands Action Area Report is the result of the study carried out by Ahrends Burton and Koralek jointly with a Warrington New Town Development Corporation multi-disciplinary team. Callands is an extension of our work at Basildon and integrates at a large scale our thinking on housing. It shows a method for building private and local authority housing both in a new development. It studies the positive contribution of landscape to the idea of a new village with its own identity within a new town. It develops further the social mix concepts carried out so successfully in Felmore and also develops our proposals for energy conservation.

Client
Warrington New Town
Development Corporation
Chief Architect & Planner
H Cannings
Chief Engineer
T Walsh, Warrington New Town
Low Energy Consultants
Ove Arup & Partners

Gross Area 960,000 m^2
Area 1 Housing 46,000 m^2

General layout plan

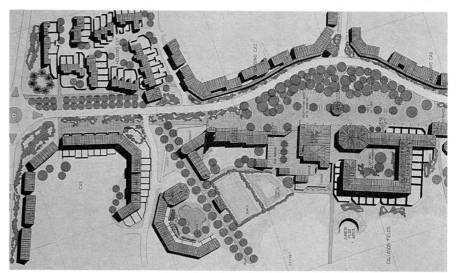

Plan of local centre

Sketch of local centre

116

Oldenburg
West Germany

Development Plan & Town Hall
Competition Entry

1979

Oldenburg is a delightful small town in North Germany.
In 1979 the City Authorities decided to hold an open ideas
competition for the replanning of an ill-defined and traffic-
blighted historic open space just beyond the city wall.
Ideas were sought for this space together with architectural
proposals for a new Town Hall and municipal offices. We
were specially invited to participate as one foreign practice
amongst several local architects to submit our design
proposals. The planning ideas that we proposed were
awarded a place in a special category.

Client
Oldenburg Stadt
Structural Engineers
Ove Arup & Partners

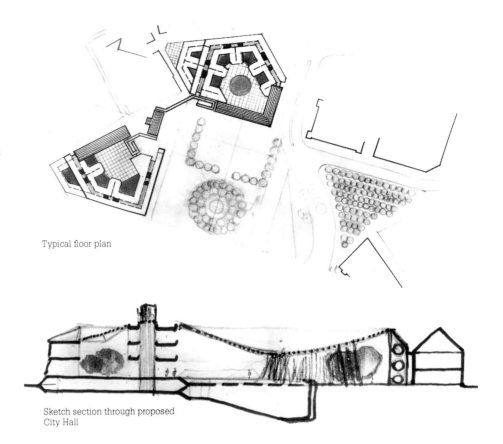

Typical floor plan

Sketch section through proposed
City Hall

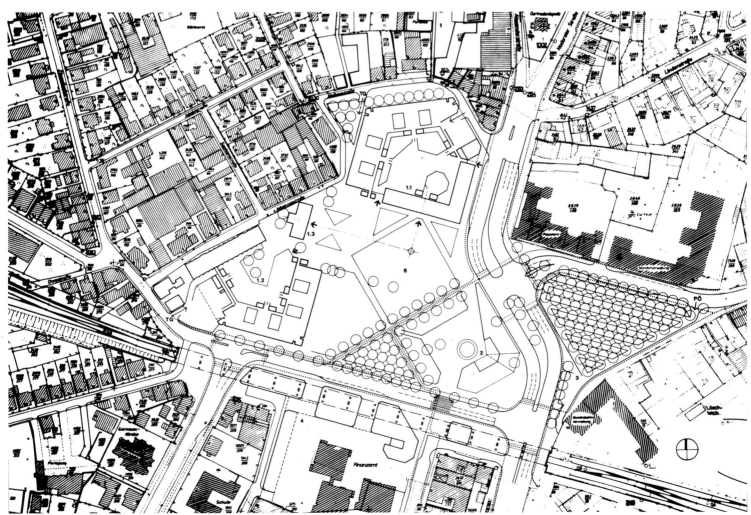

Context and general landscaping plan

John Lewis
Kingston-upon-Thames

Department Store

1979-1990

This new Department Store for the John Lewis Partnership on the Horsefair Site in Kingston takes its inspiration from the spectacular Department Stores of the 19th Century like 'Le Printemps' and 'Bonmarche'. The scheme also includes some lettable office and retail space, catering accommodation on the riverside, and basement parking for 700 cars.

The site lies between Bentalls and the River Thames, immediately to the north of Kingston Bridge. It forms a link between the town's central shopping area and the river and it fronts onto the conservation area around All Saints Church.

Our design creates an integrated and coherent development of the whole of this important site which makes a major contribution to central Kingston. The relief road, which diverts traffic to and from Kingston Bridge around the centre of the town, is incorporated into the scheme in a positive way, establishing a diagonal axis across the site which forms an underlying geometric basis for the whole design. The proposed development extends both over and under the relief road to provide a single building and creating a powerful link between the pedestrian shopping area and the river. The river frontage is developed as an extension of the existing riverside walk.

Our design is based on the formation of a very large, daylit central space within and around which the department store is planned in the form of terraced sales floors which are linked by avenues of escalators and which also extend to overlook the river. The large glazed roof, designed to carefully control the daylight, forms the main feature of the scheme. The central area is surrounded by smaller structures, clad in brick and relating to the scale of the surrounding streets.

Construction started in September 1986 and was completed in September 1990.

Client
The John Lewis Partnership
Architect
Ahrends Burton & Koralek
Structural Engineer
Ove Arup & Partners
Services Engineer
The John Lewis Partnership

Quantity Surveyor
Davis, Belfield & Everest
Project Co-ordinator
Clarson Goff Associates
Area 60,000 m²
(Gross area incl. car park)
Area 32,000 m² retail

Floor plans
1 Car park
2 Entrance to car park
3 Vehicle yard
4 Storage
5 Waitrose sales area
6 Lettable areas
7 Partners' (staff) accommodation
8 John Lewis sales area
9 Administration offices
10 Plant

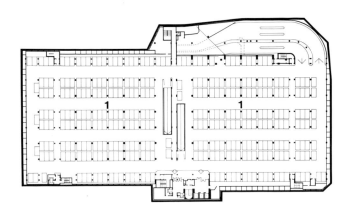

Upper level car park

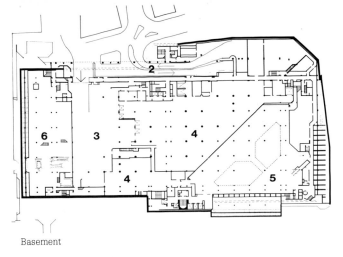

Basement

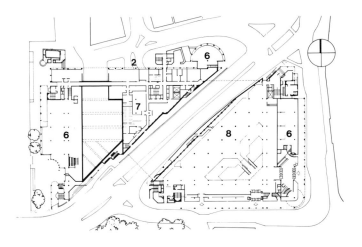

Ground floor

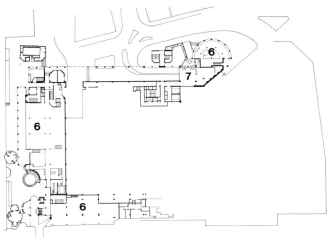

Partners' entrance and riverside walk

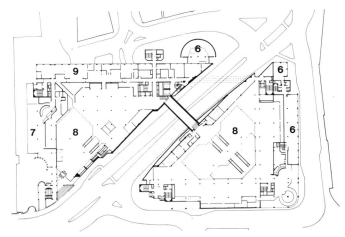

First floor

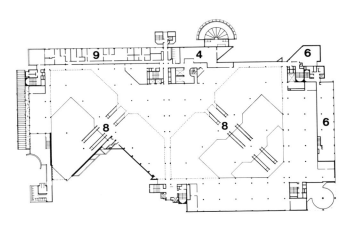

Second floor

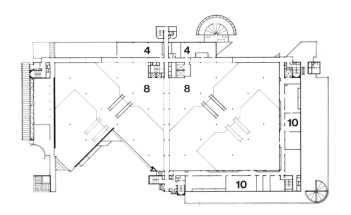

Third floor

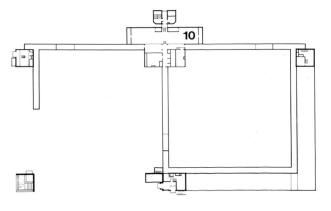

Fourth floor

West elevation from across the Thames with Kingston Bridge

Southwest entrance

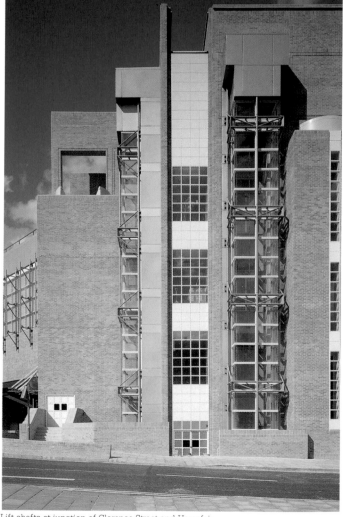

Lift shafts at junction of Clarence Street and Horsefair

Brick details

Coffee shop corner

Main interior

View up to roof from Waitrose

122

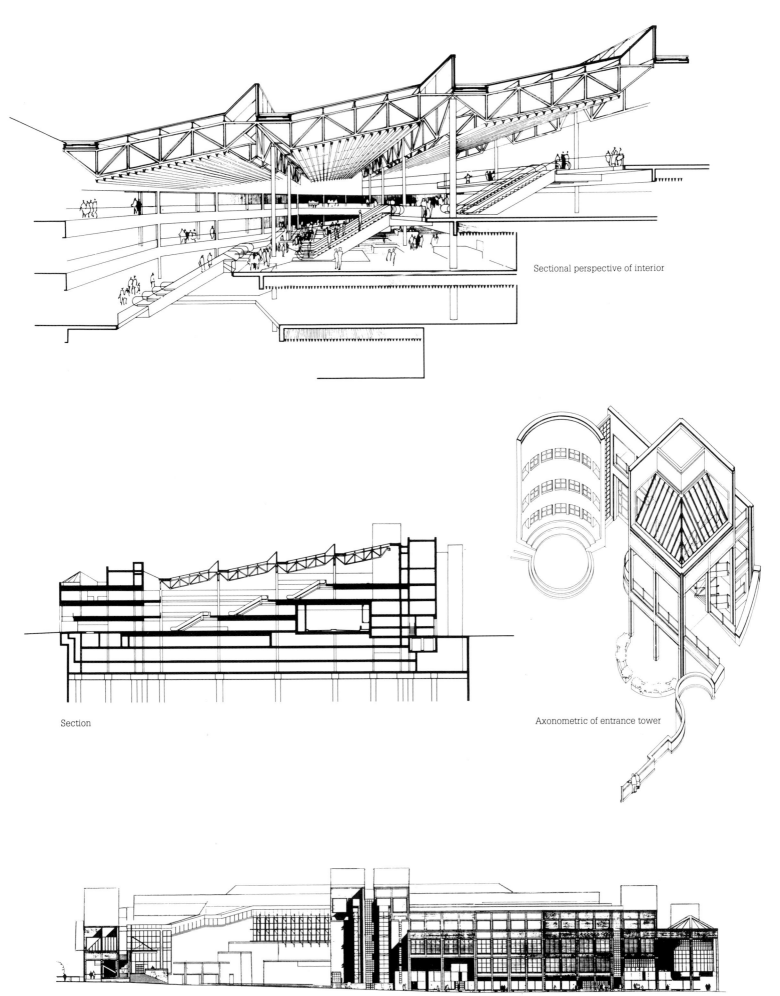

Sectional perspective of interior

Section

Axonometric of entrance tower

South elevation

123

Mary Rose Ship Museum
Portsmouth

Project

1980

This museum was designed to contain and display the
recovered hull of King Henry VIII's flagship, the Mary Rose,
which was sunk in battle in 1545 between Portsmouth and the
Isle of Wight. The development on a coastal site at Eastney on
the outskirts of Portsmouth was conceived as a major new
museum including specialist conservation workshops,
libraries, conference facilities and visitor amenities to cater for
a potential flow of a million visitors a year.

Client
Mary Rose Trust

Structural Engineer
F.J. Samuely & Partners

Building Services Engineer
Zisman Bowyer & Partners

Landscape Architect
Landesign

Design
Robin Wade Design Associates

Quantity Surveyor
Monk Dunstone & Partners

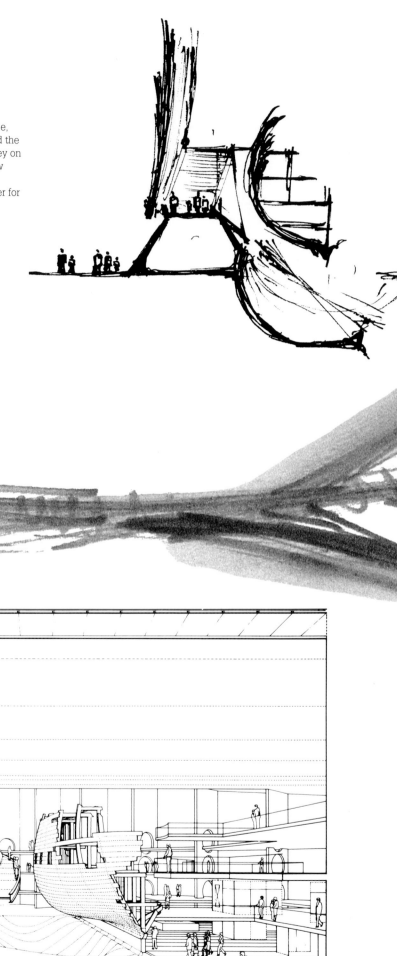

Sectional perspective of ship hall and exhibition area

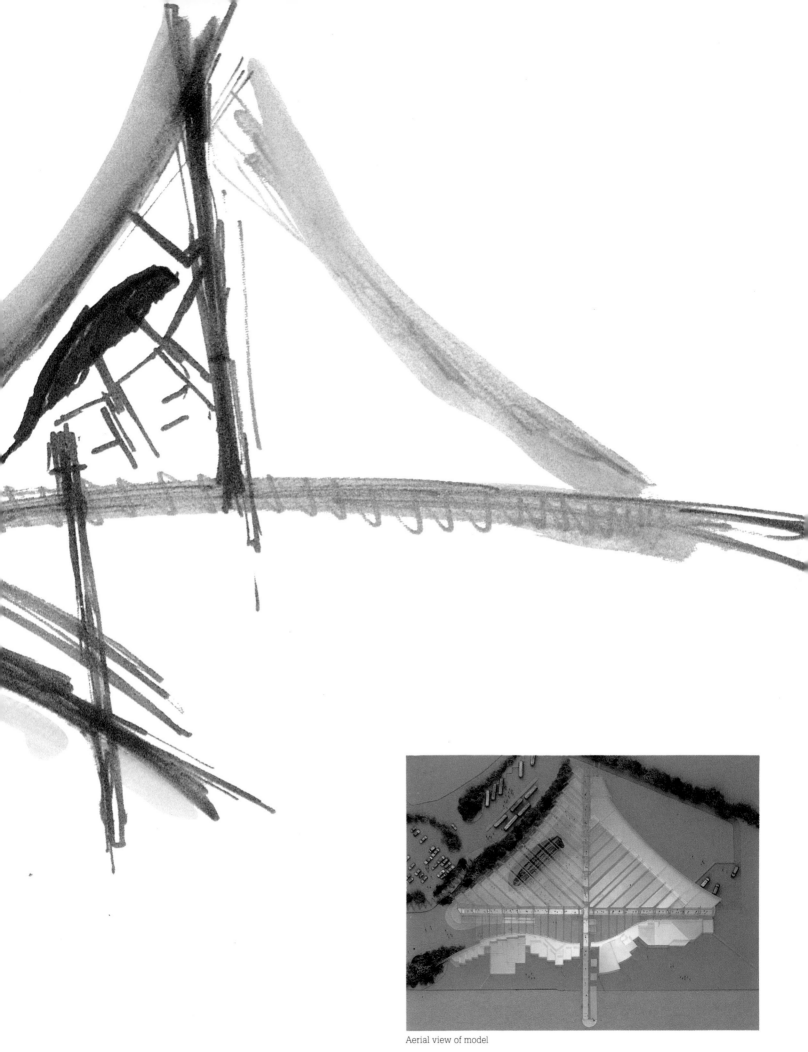

Aerial view of model

Abbey National Housing
Crystal Palace, London

Competition

1981

This scheme was submitted in an open competition sponsored by Abbey National for a mixed housing development on a site near Crystal Palace in South London.

The design was a re-interpretation of the typical London 'Mews' – informal routes for vehicular and pedestrian access, serving approximately 50 small housing units ranging from two bedroom houses to bedsitting rooms, estimated to cost between £25,000 and £15,000 per unit.

Construction was to be of brick and timber frame. Low energy use was to be assured by good insulation and controlled ventilation with a contribution from passive solar gain. Orietnation was based on consideration of the thermal implications as well as exclusion of traffic noise and the very attractive views from the site.

Client
Abbey National Building Society
Structural & Services Engineers
Ove Arup & Partners
Quantity Surveyor
Dearle & Henderson

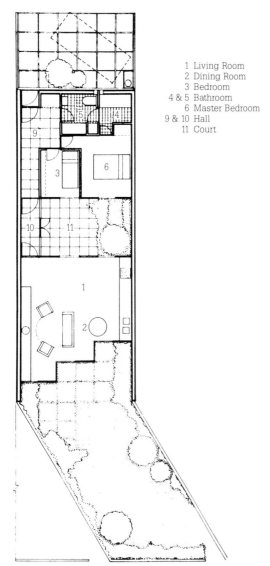

1 Living Room
2 Dining Room
3 Bedroom
4 & 5 Bathroom
6 Master Bedroom
9 & 10 Hall
11 Court

Plan of single storey house

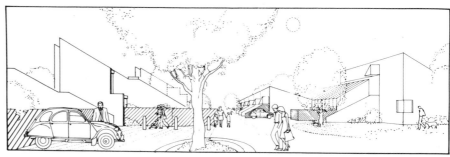

Perspective of main access route

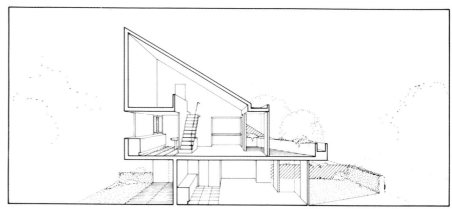

Section through two storey house

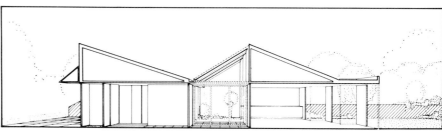

Section through single storey house

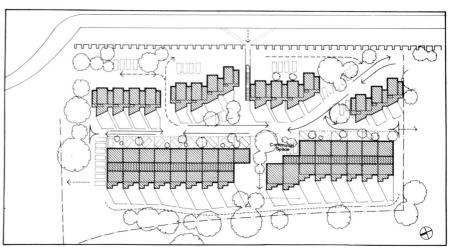

Layout plan

Thames Project

1983

This project was intended to demonstrate the importance of linking the North and South banks of the Thames at Hungerford Bridge and to promote a general revitalisation of the Thames in this area. It was initially a self generated project carried out in association with Richard Rogers and John Hawkes. Subsequently the Times newspaper asked Ahrends Burton and Koralek to give their views on the development of Lambeth and this enabled us to place our proposals in a wider context. Many of the ideas have since been taken up by others as the overall aim is becoming more widely accepted.

The principal proposals include a commercial development over Charing Cross station, the provision of a tourist tower and centre on the Embankment and the reconstruction of Hungerford Bridge with a travelator to Waterloo Station, the redevelopment of Waterloo Station, and a substantial replanning of Lambeth centering on St. George's Circus with a radial boulevard development.

Planning Consultant
John Hawkes
Quantity Surveyors
Monk Dunstone Associates
Transport Consultant
Brian Richards

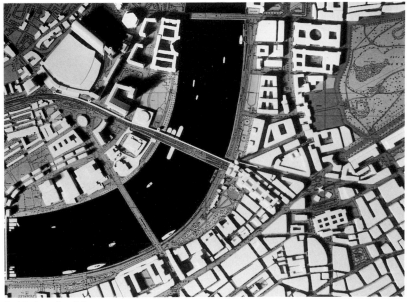

Aerial view of model

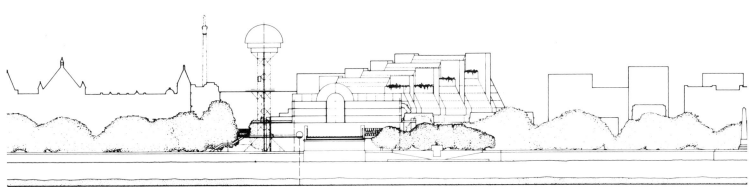

Elevation of Charing Cross from the river

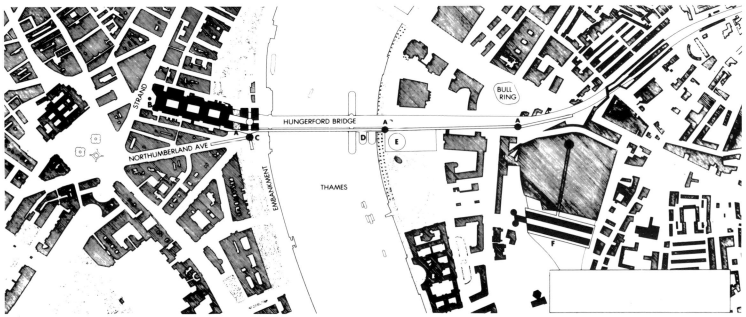

Site plan

Long view

St. Mary's Hospital
Newport, Isle of Wight

Nucleus Low Energy Hospital

1982-1990

Arising out of an energy conservation study of the Nucleus hospital system commissioned by the Department of Health in 1981, this building is the first of a new generation of 'Low Energy Nucleus' hospitals. The geometry of the plan connects the new main entrance by way of a curved circulation 'street' with the main route through the existing hospital. The Nucleus templates containing the wards and other hospital departments radiate from the curved form of the street. Garden courts, each based on a particular landscaping theme, are located between the templates. The energy centre is placed at the most advantageous point for service distribution and heat recovery purposes.

Research shows that beauty, both natural and man-made, plays an important part in speeding recovery from illness. Thus the design for all areas of the hospital and its many gardens have included provision for the arts – painting, craft, music and live entertainment.

The outer fabric of the building is designed to produce a high insulation value for both walls and roof, to provide a maintenance-free outer skin and to reduce air infiltration to an absolute minimum.

A saving of over 50% of the running cost of other similar hospitals is anticipated.

Client
DHSS Directorate of Development
Wessex Regional Health Authority
Structural Engineer
Gifford & Partners

M & E Services Engineer
Building Design Partnership
Quantity Surveyor
Building Design Partnership
Landscape Architect
Landesign Group
Area 13,500 m²

Site plan

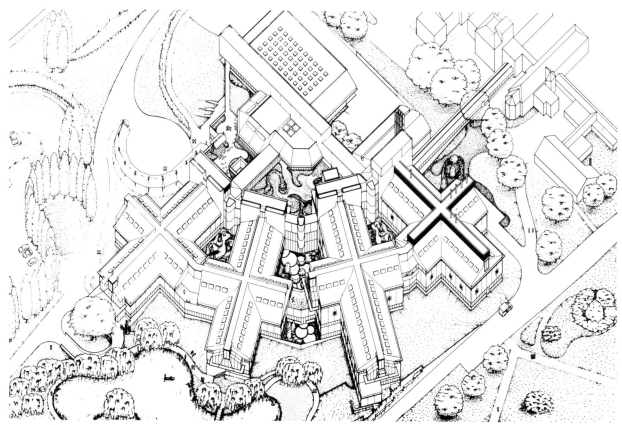

Axonometric

Aerial view

External views

National Gallery Extension

Trafalgar Square, London

1982-1985

The first of these schemes is our competition winning design for the National Gallery/Hampton Site, on Trafalgar Square. The building was to accommodate an extension to the National Gallery to house the early Renaissance collection in galleries on the daylit top floor, with three levels of commercial offices below.

This scheme was subsequently amended and eventually recast to meet a revised brief. This gave rise to a considerably larger building which nevertheless followed a similar design organisation. The application for Planning Permission was called in by the Secretary of State who refused permission in spite of a favourable report by the Inquiry Inspector, following the well known intervention by the Prince of Wales.

Both designs were low rise in their building mass with respect to the scale and character of the historic surroundings. The buildings were to be clad in stone to integrate with the National Gallery and other neighbouring buildings.

Client
Trafalgar House
Development Ltd.

Property Services Agency

Structural Engineer
S.B. Tietz and Partners

M & E Engineer
Steensen Varming
Mulcahy & Ptnrs.

Quantity Surveyor
Monk & Dunstone
Mahon & Scears

Area 8,500 m²

Site plan – competition winning scheme

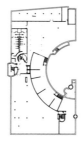
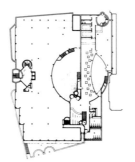
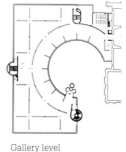

Floor plans · Gallery level · Roof

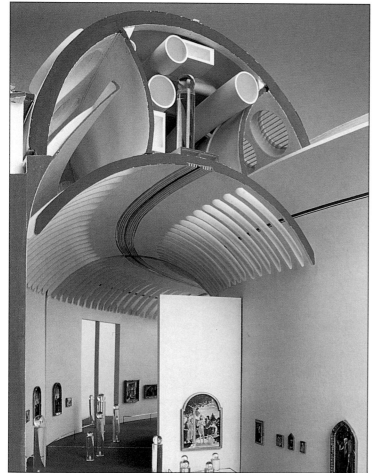

Interior model of curved Main Gallery showing service zone in the roof

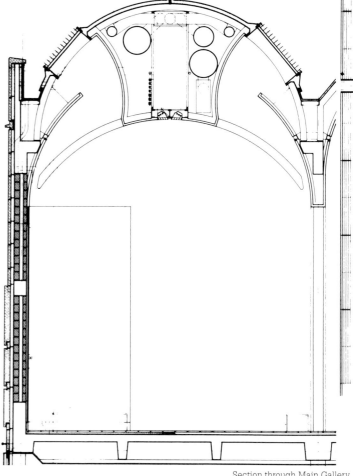

Section through Main Gallery

134

View of model as seen from Trafalgar Square

Model of competition winning scheme

Interior model of typical gallery,
amended scheme

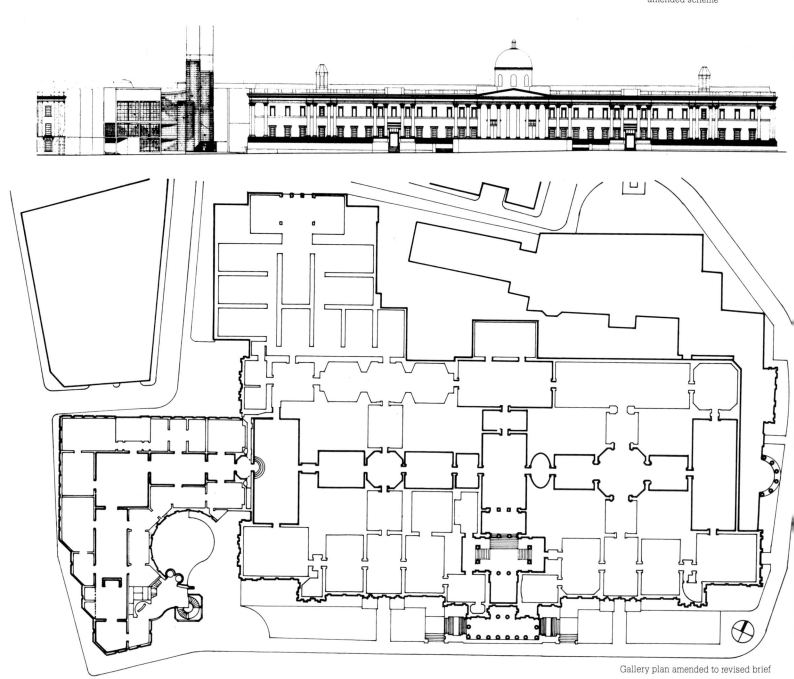

Gallery plan amended to revised brief

Model of amended scheme

W. H. Smith
Greenbridge, Swindon

Extension to the Retail Group Headquarters Building

1982-1985

The plan takes the form of a two storey matrix providing a grid of flexible office accommodation on ground and first floors and surrounding landscaped courtyards. This matrix is served by a diagonal route leading to the reception drum, the main entrance and a bridge link to the existing W.H. Smith premises.

Energy conservation considerations have led to a naturally ventilated building. Automatic external roller blinds control solar heat gain. Energy efficient uplighters provide general illumination, supplemented by desk mounted task lights.

This building was designed and built within three years and completed to the original budget and programme.

Award
1987 Financial Times Architecture at Work Award
Commendation

Client
W.H. Smith & Son Ltd.
Structural Engineer
Anthony Hunt Associates
M & E Engineers
Steensen Varming Mulcahy & Ptnrs.

Quantity Surveyor
Cyril Sweett & Ptnrs
Landscape Architects
Landesign Group
Area 4,000 m²

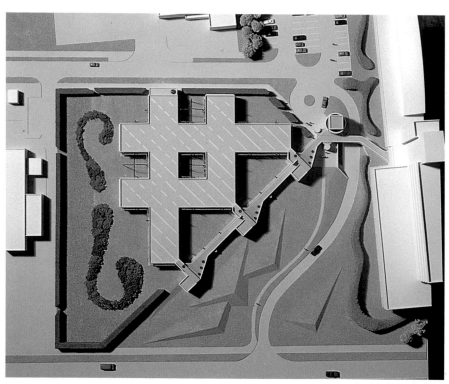

Aerial view of model

Approach to main entrance

Office areas with external blinds and sun shading

Main entrance from car park   Interior of access route to office areas

Detail of sunshading

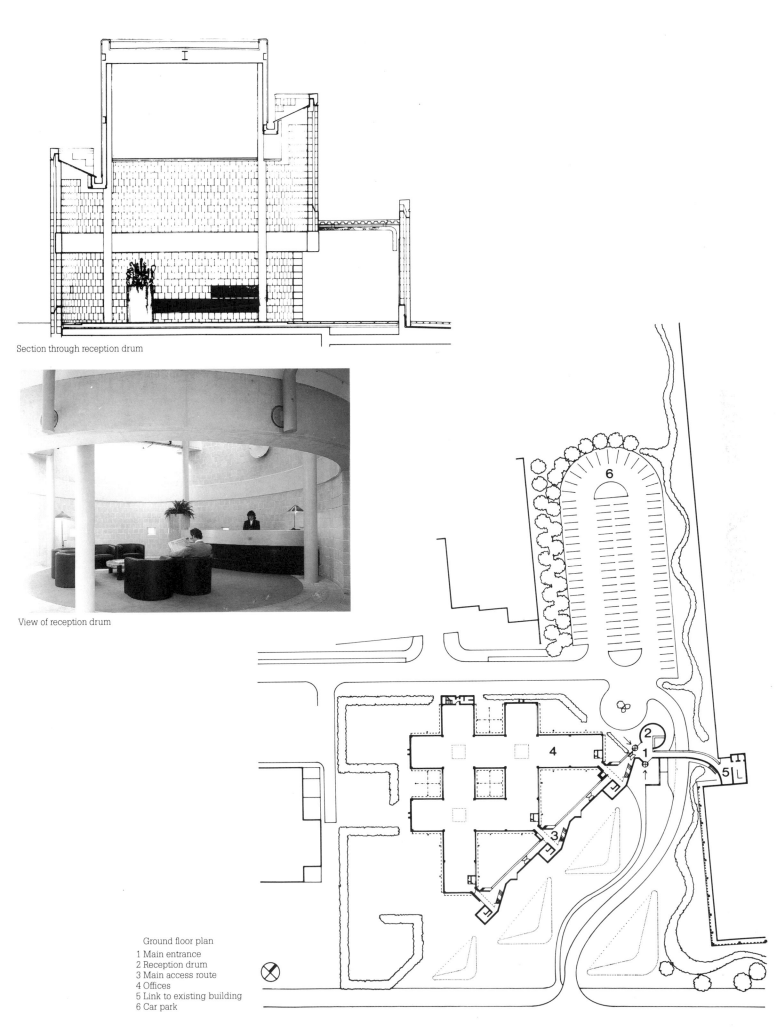

Section through reception drum

View of reception drum

Ground floor plan

1 Main entrance
2 Reception drum
3 Main access route
4 Offices
5 Link to existing building
6 Car park

J. Sainsbury

Canterbury

Supermarket

1982-1984

Our design for a new supermarket in Canterbury was the winning entry in a limited competition promoted by Sainsbury's in 1982.

The site lies to the east of the city centre with open views of the city dominated by the cathedral. The building consists of three linked clear span spaces for sales, storage and preparation and goods receiving. Flat roofs are supported on slender steel beams which are suspended from tubular steel masts by stayed tie rods. The silver coloured masts and ties give height and vertical emphasis to an otherwise low-lying building on a rather featureless site and provide a visual echo of the tower and pinnacles of the distant cathedral. They are perhaps a twentieth century equivalent of the same principles of highly stressed minimal structure.

The shop front, which faces onto a large open car park, is clad in square aluminium and glass panels. A teflon-coated fabric canopy is suspended from the mast stays along the length of the shopfront terminating in a quadrant at the entrance lobby which is supported from a central mast giving visual emphasis to the main entrance.

Awards
1985 Structural Steel Design Award
1986 Civic Trust Award
1986 Financial Times Architecture at Work Commendation

Client	Services Engineer
J. Sainsbury plc	J. Sainsbury plc
Architects for the fitting out	Quantity Surveyor
J. Sainsbury plc	Henry Riley & Son
Structural Consultant, Competition Stage	Area approximately 4,000 m²
Anthony Hunt Associates	
Structural Engineer	
Ernest Green & Partners	

Main elevation towards car park

Entrance canopy

143

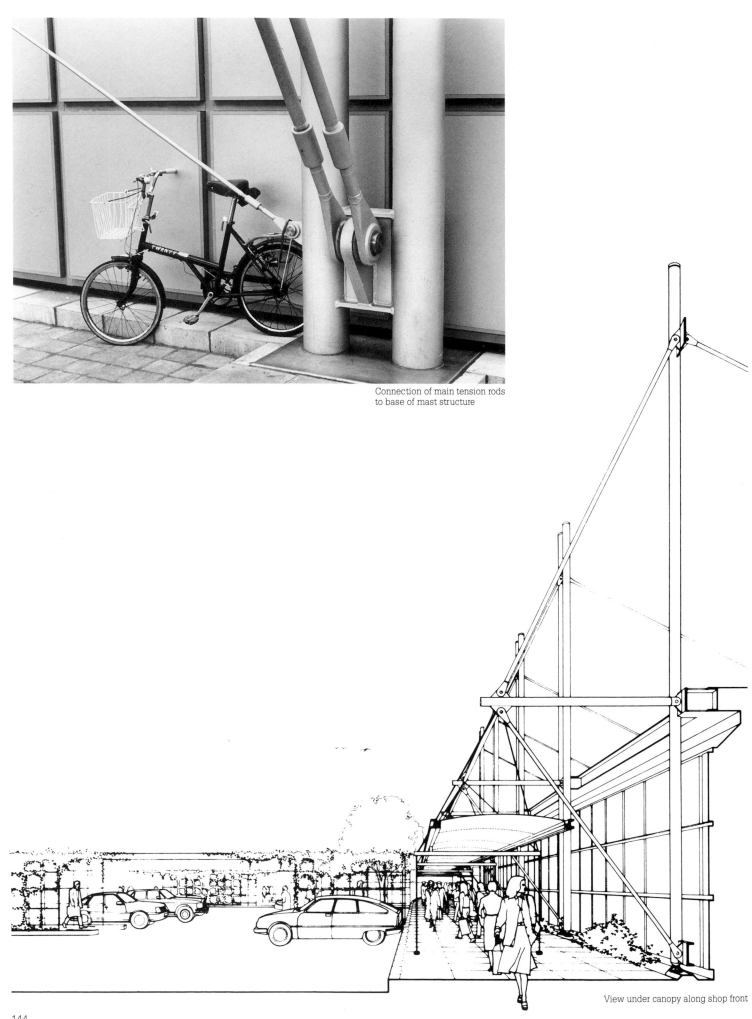

Connection of main tension rods
to base of mast structure

View under canopy along shop front

144

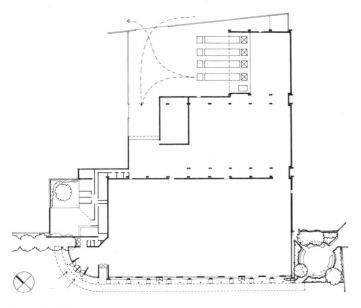

Ground floor plan

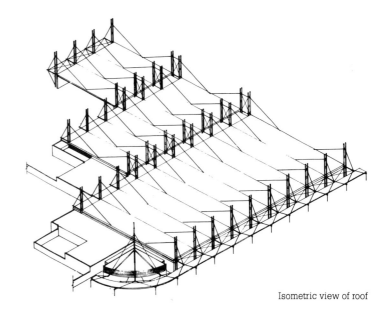

Isometric view of roof

Elevation from the car park

Hooke Park College
Dorset

School for advanced manufacturing in wood

1983

The building is set in a 350 acre area of woodland five miles from the School for Craftsmen in Wood at Parnham House. Three distinct types of building house the separate functions of the college – Workshop, Public Building, School Residences. They are integrated into the forest landscape. Each building form explores various structural solutions and utilises the properties of unsawn round timber in a new interpretation of timber technology.

Public access is provided by an observation gallery over the Workshop which allows the public to view the processes of production and to pass through to the Public Interpretation Centre and Dining Room. The Public Building will also provide a focus in the forest for a system of walks and trails through the forest.

The prototype incorporates the principal structural techniques, both tension and compress, developed for this project and was constructed under the direct supervision of this office. At present an offices and teaching building it will eventually be used as staff accommodation. The innovative use of high-technology epoxy resin in a relatively small application at the joints of a low-technology material timber has liberated people's imagination as a new method of construction using traditional material can be foreseen.

The workshop structure is formed of three shells using a 15m arch of wet roundwood in compression. The shell is covered in a double skin PVC coated membrane roof and is 600 m² in area.

The Parnham Trust, under the directorship of John Makepeace, plans to exploit the considerable potential of an otherwise wasted raw material, forest thinnings. The creation of the college utilises this resource by providing a training in the design, manufacture and marketing of high-quality new products from round unsawn timber.

Awards
1987 PA Innovation in Building Design and Construction (shortlisted)
1990 British Construction Industry Commendation

Client
The Parnham Trust
Consultant Architect
Professor Frei Otto

Structural and Services Engineer
Buro Happold
Quantity Surveyor
Bernard Williams

Prototype structure

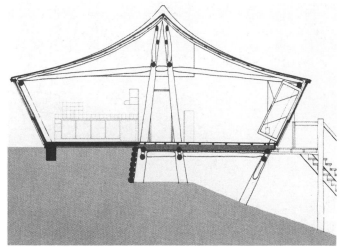

Section of prototype house

Prototype house elevation

Project model

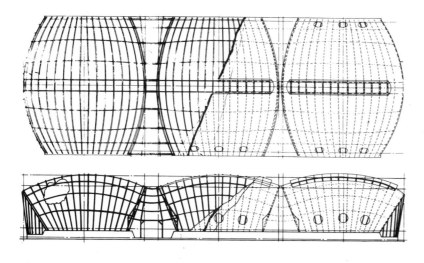

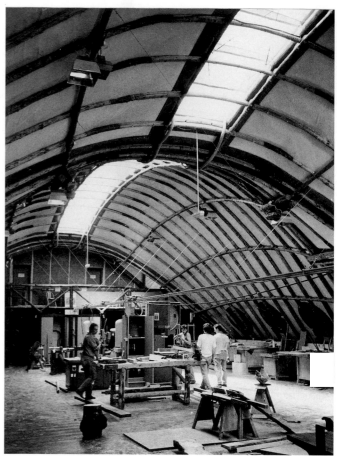

Hooke Park College Student workshop

View from west

British Telecom
Milton Keynes

Headquarters Building

Submission in limited competition

1983

This competition entry proposes the accommodation of a very large office complex within a single building, sub-divided into four pavilions and linked by a glazed pedestrian street. A fifth pavilion incorporates the main entrance and centralised facilities. Our design aims to meet the stringent demands of information technology on the office of the future, creating a new form of flexible office environment which combines the advantages of cellular and open office planning without imposing the more extreme limitations of either.

The proposed servicing systems embody a variety of important energy conserving measures which would result in energy savings of 40% by comparison with a conventional air-conditioned office building.

Client
British Telecom
Structural & Services
Engineer
Buro Happold
Quantity Surveyor
Monk Dunstone Associates
Area 32,800 m^2

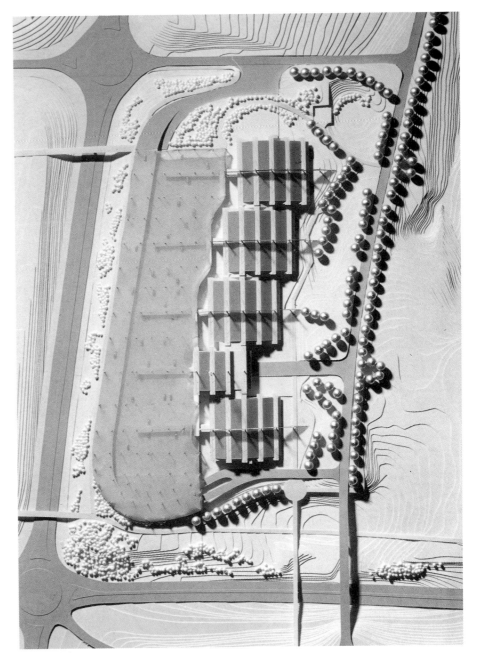

Project model

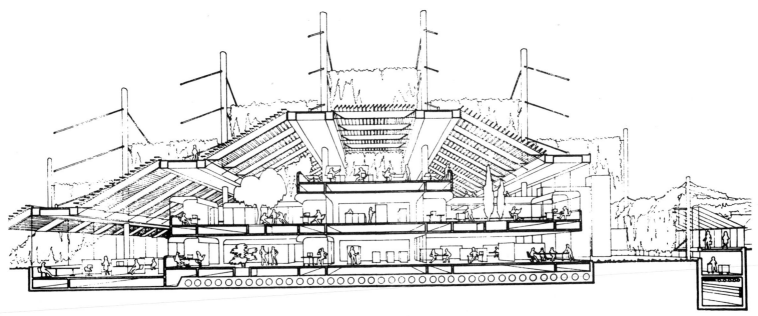

Section of offices

National Garden Festival
Stoke On Trent

Festival Hall

1985-1986

This design was the winning entry in a limited competition for the main hall for the 1986 National Garden Festival at Stoke on Trent. The Festival Hall consists of a group of white p.v.c. coated polyester fabric cones giving a festive impression adorned with flags and banners. The large cones are 28 metres square and the smaller ones 14 metres square, and are supported on lattice steel masts. The cones cover the main exhibition space which contained changing exhibitions throughout the Festival.

Client
National Garden
Festival 1986

Structural Engineers
Ove Arup & Partners

National Garden Festival
Co-ordinating Architects
Sebire Allsopp

Design Co-ordinator
Joe Samworth

Area 3,500 m²

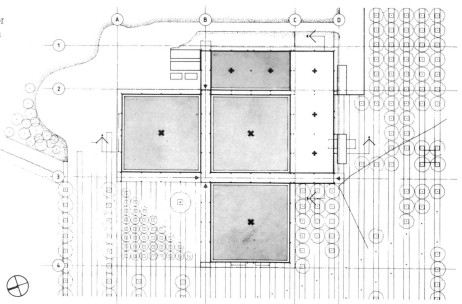

Site plan

Sketch from the lake

Brookwood Park Feasibility Study
Woking, Surrey

Project

1986

Our work on this Site Acquisition Study for a 170 acre site on the outskirts of Woking was not only a planning study for different use zones across the whole site, but also an exploration in some detail of a brief for the design of IBM offices totalling approximately 120,000 m².

Conceptual design work was carried out for low rise office buildings in seven locations on the southern part of this parkland site. Studies included preliminary work on strategies for the infrastructure, civil and structural, engineering and cost planning services, and building services.

Client
IBM (UK) Ltd
Structural Engineers
Buro Happold
M & E Engineers
Building Design Partnership
Chartered Surveyors
J.R. Eve
Chartered Surveyors
Weatherall Green & Smith

Civil Engineers
Blyth & Blyth Associates
Consulting Engineers &
Planners
Travers Morgan Planning
Quantity Surveyors
Gardiner & Theobald
Landscape Architects
Landesign Group

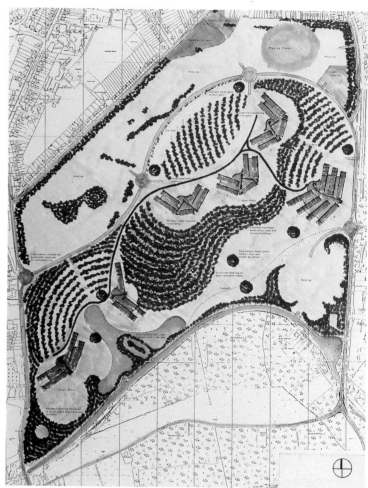

Site development plan

Sketch elevation

Perspective view of office building

152

Stoneyard Lane Development
Isle of Dogs, London

Feasibility Study

1985

This feasibility study was for a mixed development on the 1.75 hectare Stoneyard Lane site on the edge of the Isle of Dogs, to accommodate offices, flats and an extension to Hackney College, together with landscape proposals for land to the north of the Docklands Relief Road.

Our proposal establishes a coherent formal connection between the main development on the Stoneyard Lane site and the much smaller Ming Street site whilst taking into account the existing character of Poplar High Street and the very different proposed redevelopment of the Isle of Dogs.

Client
London Docklands
Development Corporation
Landscape Architects
Landesign Group

Aerial view of site development model

Burton House
Kentish Town, London
1986-1987 and 1989

This is a courtyard house formed by four structural pavilions with a linking conservatory. It proposes an alternative way of building houses in cities being itself set in the middle of a dense part of North London. It is conceived as a place in which to live and work.

The site is about 19 metres by 15 metres. The house is entered through a round gate in the boundary wall which flanks its eastern side. A glazed roof extends from end to end of the house and forms a generous porch to the front door which opens into the conservatory leading to the house and court garden. The outlook is onto the gardens and the richly articulated backs of the houses to the South.

The house itself consists of three pavilions each with a similar structure in exposed timber, one pavilion extending to a first floor to house the master bedroom and bathroom. On the ground floor, the three linked spaces of dining kitchen, sitting room and study/guest-room each have quite different atmospheres created by the varying ceiling design and use of glazing in walls and roof. Toplight is used throughout in varying ways.

The studio/guesthouse pavilion has a single volume with the guest gallery in it.

The design takes a middle path view of energy conservation with comfort and delight playing their important parts in this aspect. Natural light, passive solar gain and very good insulation are combined to contribute to the solution. The main materials are timber for structure, brick for walls and floors, glass and anodised aluminium for cladding and windows.

The house incorporates works of art and craft both in its fabric and garden. Stuart Hill, Bill Pye, James Hope, Jupp Dernbach and James Sutton have contributed, and much of the joinery in the house has been made by Mark and Bim Burton.

Client
Richard and Mireille Burton
Structural & Environmental Engineers
Ove Arup & Partners
Contractor
Stronghold Engineering & Construction with John Yates

Area of house 167 m²
Area of studio/guest house 87 m²

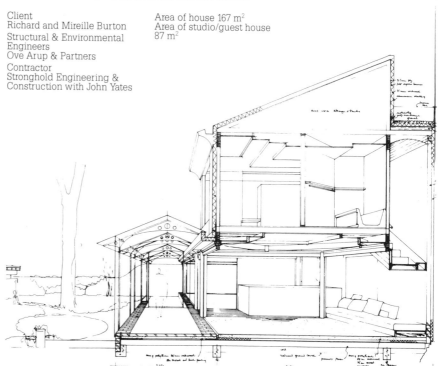

Sketch section

Dining and kitchen

View of entrance from conservatory

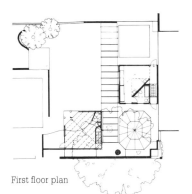

First floor plan

Ground floor plan

Elevation from Lady Margaret Road

179 Shaftesbury Avenue
London

Central London Office Development

1986

This building is designed to take maximum advantage of the site within a height constraint which arises in relation to daylighting rights to adjacent buildings. Service cores are situated at each end of the deep plan office space.

Formally the building expresses its position at the north end of Shaftesbury Avenue as a gateway to the West End. The architectural language developed recognises and presents two distinct faces; the more formal and substantial vertical face which addresses Shaftesbury Avenue, and the curved lightweight cladding in response to the smaller residential buildings on New Compton Street to the west.

The building is air conditioned with basement plant lying beneath the basement car park, with the main air distribution ducts forming a part of the lightweight cladding system.

Client
Standard Life
Assurance Co.
Structural Engineers
Ove Arup & Partners
M & E Engineers
Ferguson & Partners
Space Planning
Consultants
DEGW
Area 12,600 m²

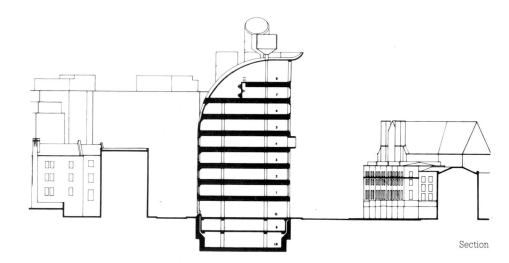

Section

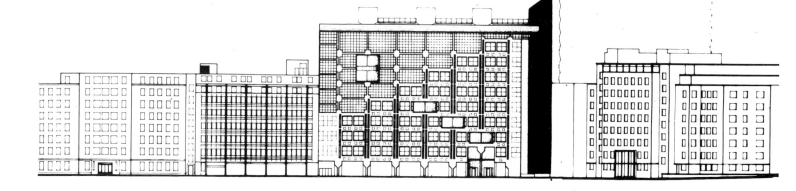

East elevation

156

Floor plans

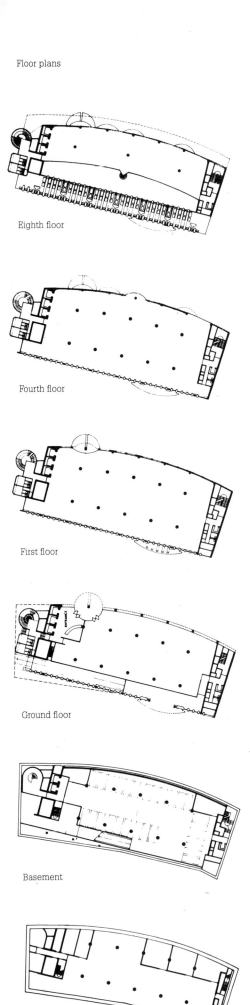

Eighth floor

Fourth floor

First floor

Ground floor

Basement

Lower basement

Elevation from the north east

157

Stag Place Competition
Victoria, London

2 Competitions on adjacent sites for urban redevelopment for offices on site A, and environmental improvement on site B.

1987

Our Competition A proposal for a new office building has been guided by three main objectives:

To re-establish Bressenden Place as a street, we have planned the line of the building to follow the curve of the street and continue this curve towards Portland House, by means of an extended entrance canopy.

To respond sympathetically to the great difference in height and character between adjacent buildings, we have created a stepped building as a visual bridge between them.

To provide the Victoria area with a building which has a strong presence and makes a contribution both at a formal and social level, we have designed a configuration with two wings enclosing a covered court accommodating a variety of recreational and catering spaces.

Our Competition B proposal is for a Leisure Pool complex covered by large glazed roof structures which would create sculptural and yet transparent forms within the space of the square. These roofs provide a sheltered and pleasant environment for pedestrians as well as providing visual interest at ground level and when viewed from above from the surrounding buildings.

Client
Land Securities plc
Structural Engineers
Ove Arup & Partners
Services Engineers
Ove Arup & Partners
Quantity Surveyors
Monk Dunstone Associates
Gross areas A 29,000 m²
B 3,716 m²

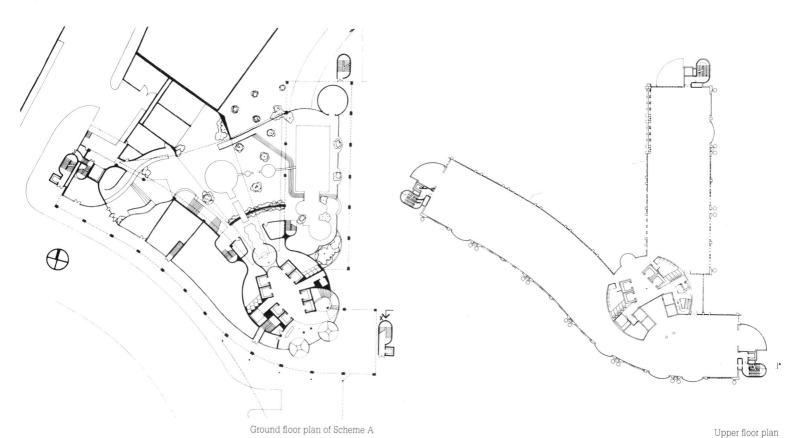

Ground floor plan of Scheme A

Upper floor plan

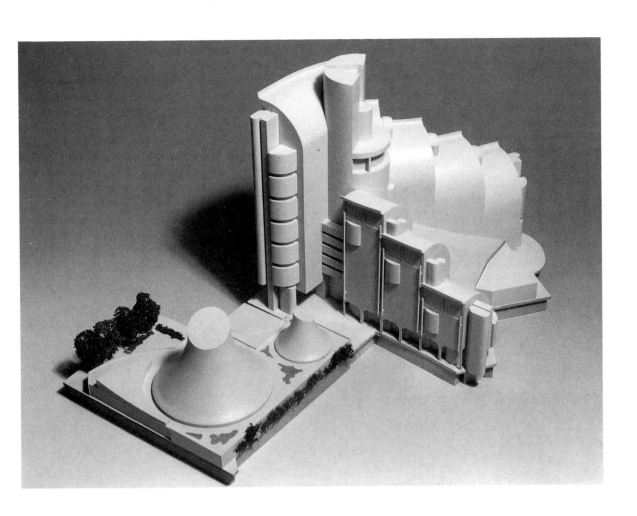

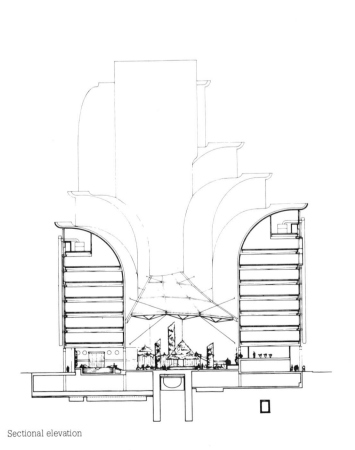

Sectional elevation

View along Bressenden Place

Docklands Light Railway
East London

Light Railway Stations

1987

When the eastern extension of the Docklands Light Railway was in its early stages of design, the London Docklands Development Corporation recognised the need to view the stations as part of their context, and not simply as isolated events. The LDDC decided to seek architects on a competitive basis to pursue both the station designs and their links into the surrounding infrastructure, and we were awarded this commission in October 1987.

From the outset we have worked closely with the LDDC, DLR and their project engineers, G. Maunsell & Partners, and with developers for adjacent sites in order to advance both aspects of the Brief simultaneously.

Our work on the context to the stations has led to the identification of the need for specific projects to complete the links between the stations and surrounding development, and we continue to be involved in certain of these projects.

The concept for the stations is essentially that of a kit of parts which is applied to each station. However, due to constraints of the context such as crossing of road corridors, the stations vary in their form falling into three main categories.

Viaduct stations have side platforms with access from the ground via lift and stairs.

Ground level stations generally are of island platform type, with access via a high level walkway which also serves as a public route over the tracks. Both the walkway and the platform will be accessed via lifts and stairs.

The stations at Beckton Park and Cyprus form a third category. The railway here lies between the two lanes of the Royal Albert Dock Spine Road. At these stations the road rises to a roundabout with an open centre and the railway gently falls to form the station beneath. Pedestrian access over the tracks is achieved with a footbridge crossing north south in the open centre of the station.

The proposed extension will run from Poplar eastwards through Blackwall to Canning Town and onwards to the north of the Royal Docks, terminating at Beckton.

Client
The LDDC
Structural Engineer/Services
Engineer/Quantity Surveyor
G. Maunsell & Partners

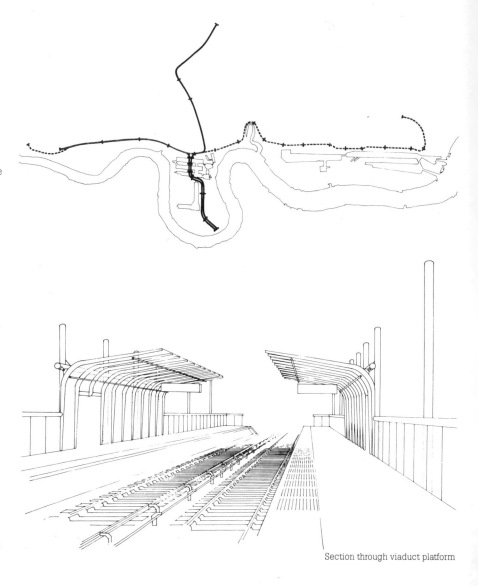

Section through viaduct platform

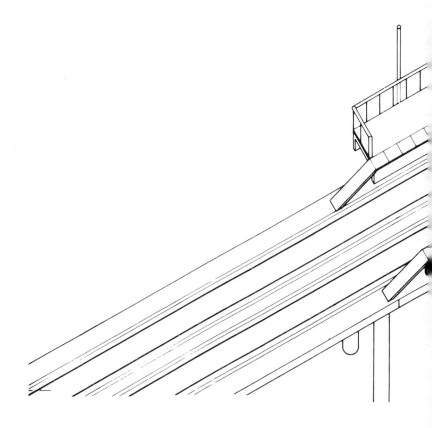

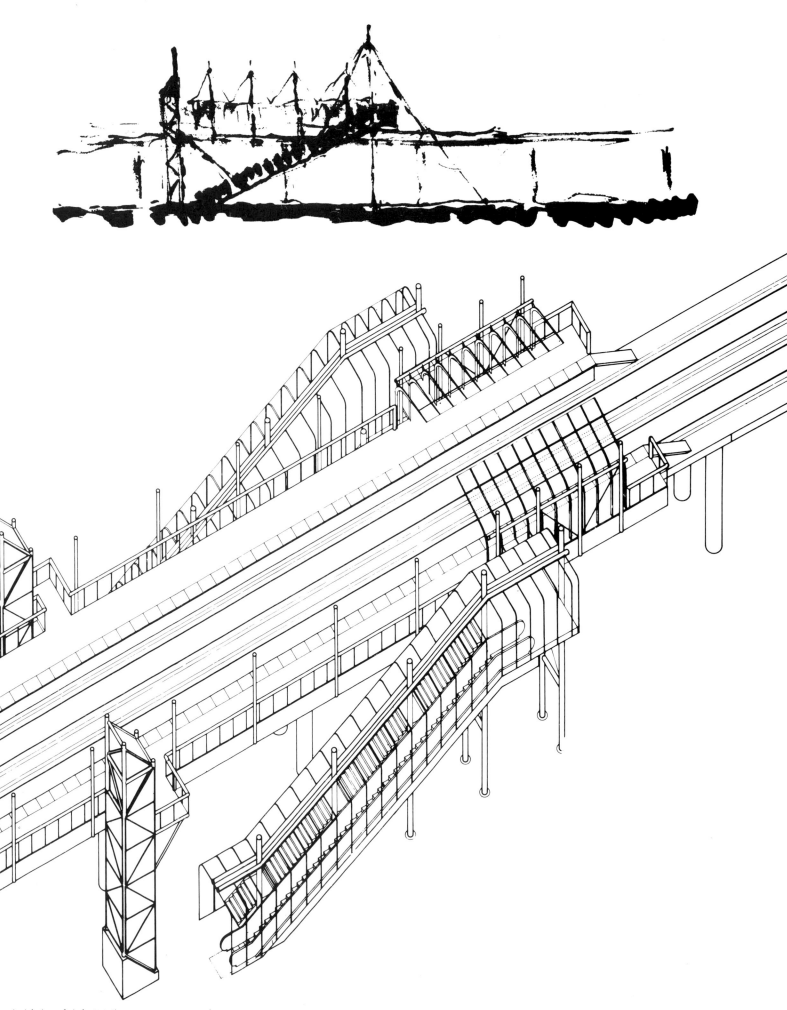

Aerial view of viaduct station

Dover Heritage Centre
Dover

The White Cliffs Experience
Exhibition spaces, Theatre, Museum, Restaurant, Craft Shops

1988-

The form of the building is derived from consideration of its location within the town, the archaeological remains on the site and the organisation of exhibition spaces for the displays in the centre.

The main approach to the building will be from Market Square and the scheme is designed around a pedestrian route leading up to and through the building from Market Square to York Street.

The building consists of two and three storey elements in grey brick with bands of light cream brick marking cornice levels and forming door and window surrounds. The 'Time and Tide' theatre is contained within a brick cylinder of similar construction. In contrast to these rather solid elements there are two delicate lightweight structures in the form of glazed crescent shaped spaces with steeply sloping glass roofs looking out onto 'archaeological gardens' displaying, on the one side, the remains of the Norman church of St Martin le Grand and, on the other, bastions of the 'classis Britanica' and 'Saxon Shore' forts.

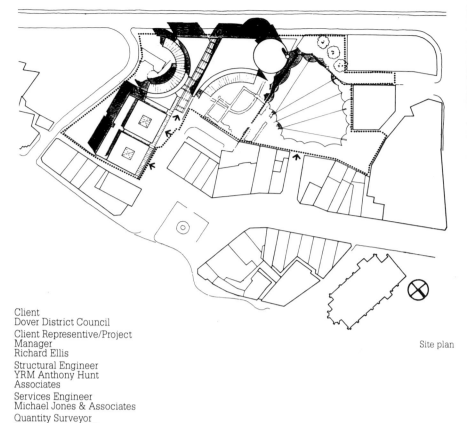

Site plan

Client
Dover District Council
Client Representive/Project Manager
Richard Ellis
Structural Engineer
YRM Anthony Hunt Associates
Services Engineer
Michael Jones & Associates
Quantity Surveyor
Davis Langdon & Everest
Management Contractor
Bovis Construction Ltd
Area 5,000 m²

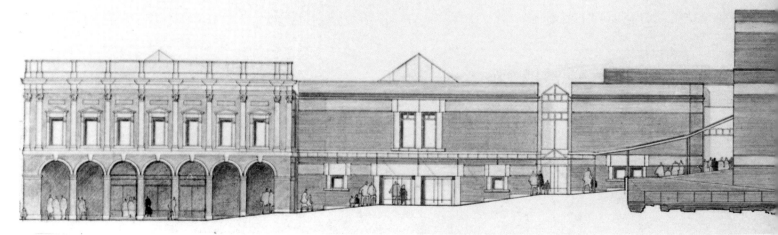

Principal elevation

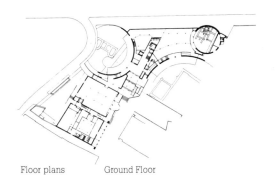
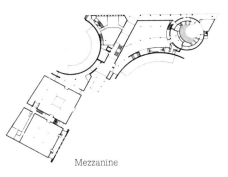
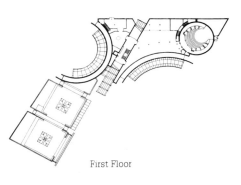

Floor plans   Ground Floor   Mezzanine   First Floor

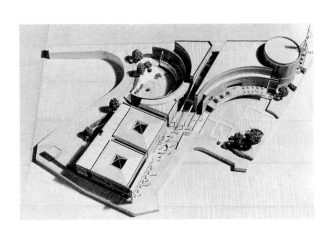

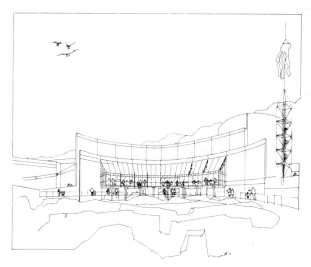

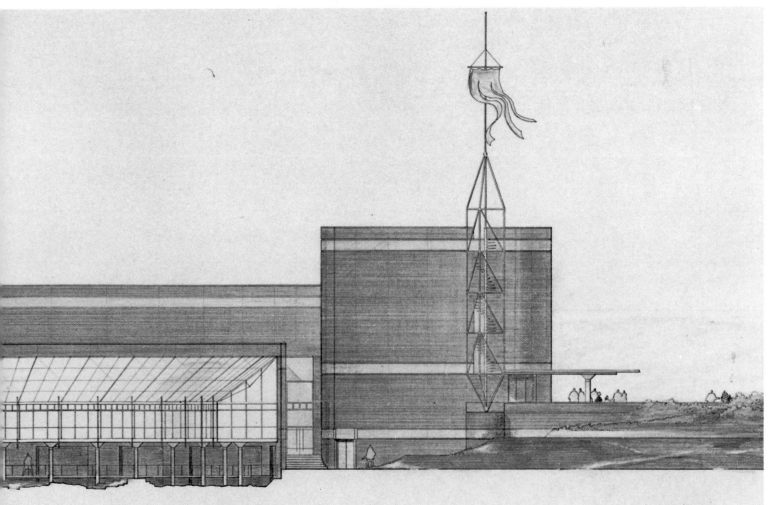

British Rail North Pole Depot
London

1989-1990

This project comprises a number of buildings as part of a major new depot to service the channel tunnel trains.

The buildings range in size from the servicing shed which is over four hundred metres long by approximately thirty-eight metres wide, to the relatively small gatehouse.

The servicing shed, which is designed to contain a maximum of six full train sets, will house the activities related to fast turn around of the trains on a daily basis.

Major aspects of train maintenance and repair will be dealt with in the repair shed, which is approximately half the size of the servicing shed, large enough to house four half train sets at one time. Both the servicing and the repair sheds have associated amenity and stores functions and these are housed adjacent to the sheds.

Client
British Rail
Structural Engineer
Ove Arup & Partners
Services Engineers
Loren Butt Consultancies
Mott MacDonald
Quantity Surveyors
Monk Dunstone Associates
Faithful & Gould
Fire Consultants
Fire Check Consultants
Storage Consultant
The Jolyon Drury Consultancy
Area 30,000 m^2 (approximate)

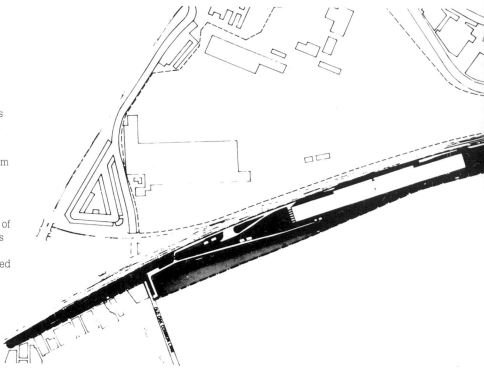

164

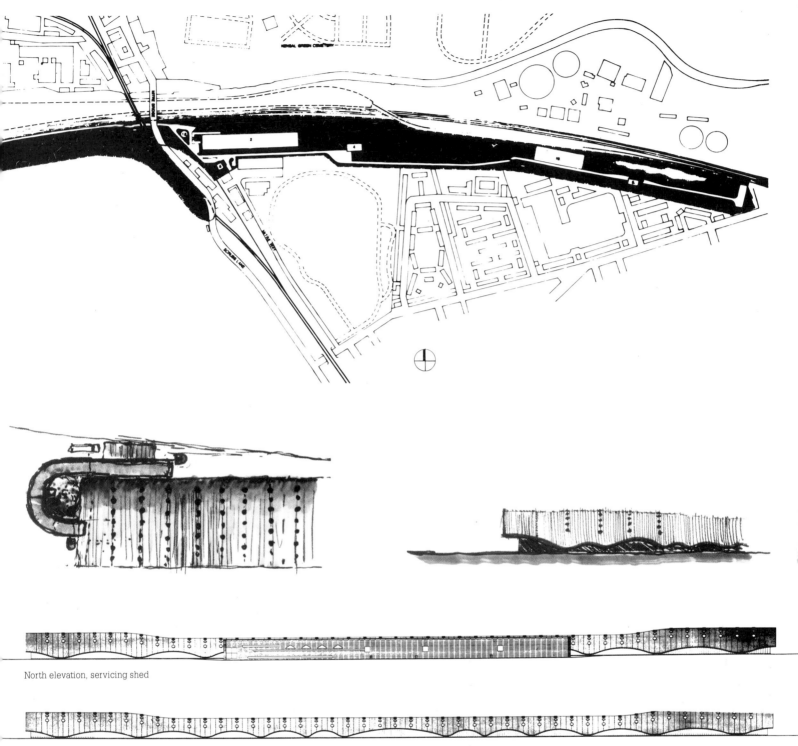

North elevation, servicing shed

South elevation, servicing shed

Cross section, servicing shed

New British Embassy
Moscow

Preliminary Design

1988-

The new site for the British Embassy is on the Smolenskaya Embankment of the Moscow River. At this point the river has a generous curve, giving the site wide views to the west. The site will accommodate the Ambassador's Suite, Chancery and other offices, reception rooms, flats for staff and their recreational facilities.

The main building addresses the river with a great timber roof forming a portico to a courtyard/garden. The flats, in two wings, front onto gardens to the north and Protochny Street to the south. The entrance to the Embassy is from Protochny Street through a porte cochère into a high covered forecourt. The main entrance leads from this into a generous entrance hall with a large bay window opening onto the courtyard garden which, in winter, will have an ice sculpture. All public offices, the restaurant and public hall have access from the entrance hall. The Ambassador's Suite, which is in a pavilion overlooking the river, is accessed by a curved stair leading from the hall through an ambulatory above. The recreational facilities are below the courtyard garden and are top lit. They consist of a swimming pool, squash court, commissariat and clubroom.

The materials proposed are light in colour in contrast to the surrounding buildings and will be stone, aluminium cladding and timber to the curved roof and columns.

Client
Foreign and Commonwealth Office
Services Engineer
Ove Arup & Partners
Services Consultant
YRM Engineers

Quantity Surveyor
Hanscomb
Landscape
Landesign
Area 9,250 m²

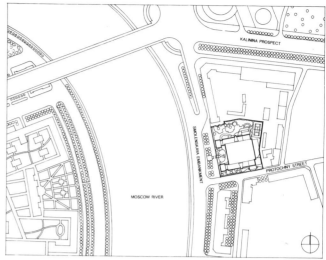
Site plan

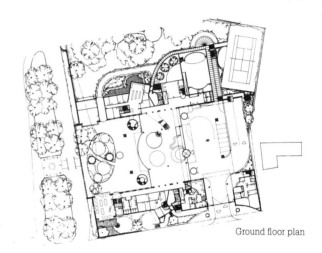
Ground floor plan

View across the Moskva River

166

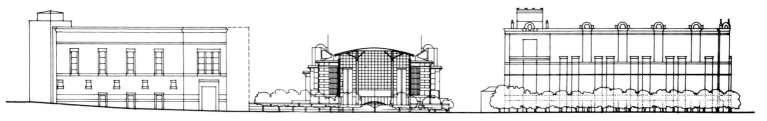

West elevation along Smolenskaya Embankment

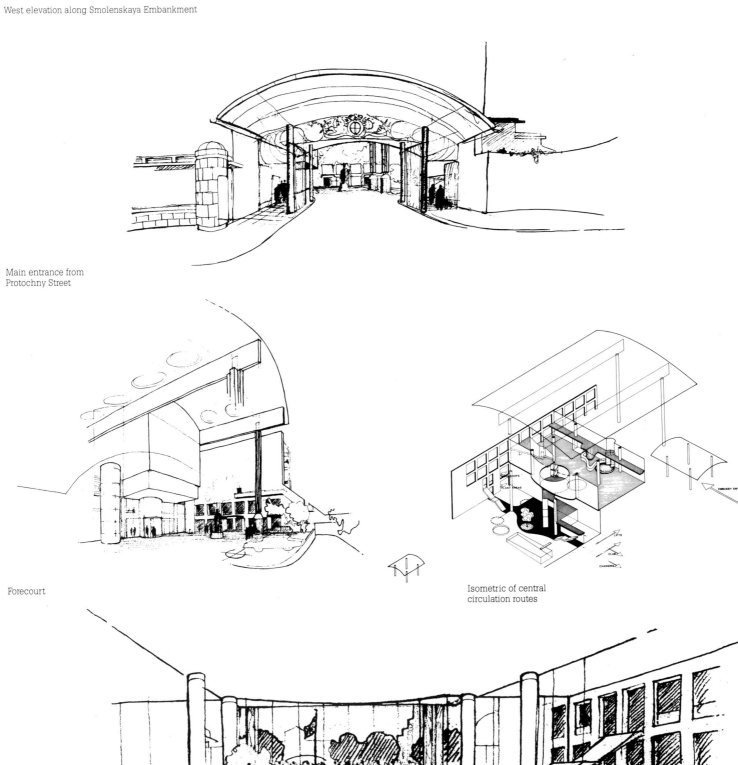

Main entrance from
Protochny Street

Forecourt

Isometric of central
circulation routes

Main entrance lobby

Compton Verney Opera House
Warwickshire

Finalist in International Competition

1989

This design was a submission in the final stage of an international competition. The brief was, firstly, to make a building that will provide a worthy setting for the unique experience offered by this exceptional opportunity and, secondly, to find a form appropriate to this beautiful site and in particular to resolve the problems of scale resulting from the construction of such a large building.

Our design aims to develop an overall concept for the whole site, integrating landscape and architecture. The mass of the building is broken down into smaller elements which relate in scale to the existing buildings and which take the form of pavilions in the landscape, a blend of formality and informality, with consistency of materials – stone and glass.

The design is a new interpretation of the traditional Opera House form – glass enclosed auditorium allowing a true sense of opera in the landscape. This enclosure would take the form of a double skin of glass and shutters which would close, as if by magic, just before a performance.

'. . . and here's a marvellous convenient place for our rehearsal. This green plot shall be our stage . . .'

Client
Compton Verney Opera
Project
Associate Architect
Professor Frei Otto
Landscape Architect
Landesign

Engineers
Buro Happold
Quantity Surveyors
Monk Dunstone Associates
Acoustic Engineers
Arup Acoustics
Area 17,200 m²

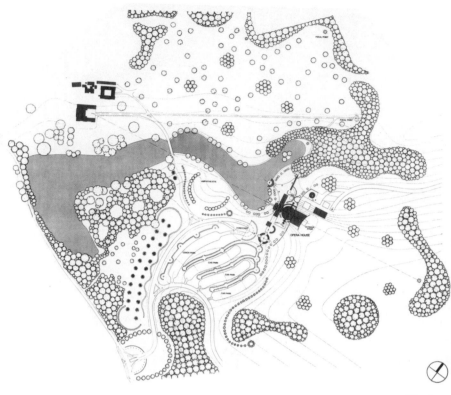

Site plan

View across the lake

168

Perspective views

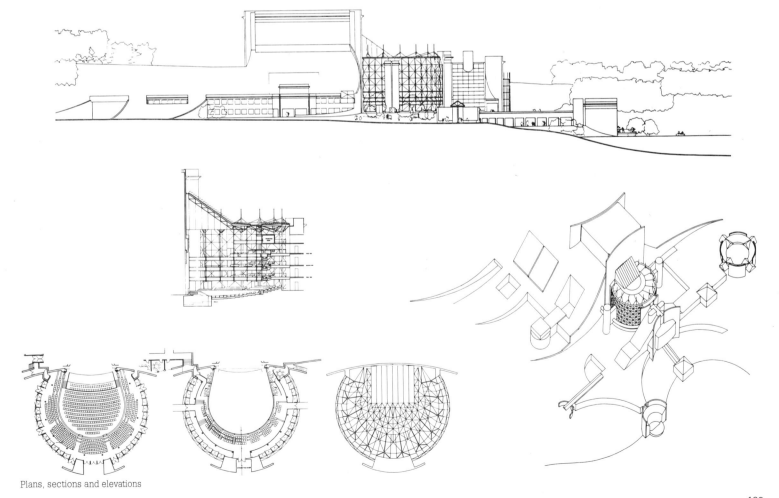

Plans, sections and elevations

Bibliography

Basildon Southwest Area Study
Official Architecture and Planning
Jul 1971

Burton House
Sunday Telegraph Magazine
3 Apr 1988
The Independent
15 Dec 1989
Sunday Times
17 Dec 1989
The Independent
20 Dec 1989
Daily Telegraph
21 Dec 1989
Guardian
13 Jan 1990
Building Design
19 Jan 1990
Ham and High
26 Jan 1990
Glass Age
Feb 1990
Architectural Review
Sep 1990

Canberra Bell Tower
Architects' Journal
8 May 1968
Architectural Design
Jun 1968
L'Architecture d'Aujourd'hui
Dec 1971/Jan 1972

Chalvedon Housing
Architectural Review
Sep 1970
RIBA Journal
Jan 1976
Le Monde
10 Feb 1976
RIBA Journal
Jan 1976
Building
Jun 1977
Architecture
Jun 1977
Baumeister
Jul 1977
Architects' Journal
14 Sep 1977
Architects' Journal
26 Oct 1977
Good Design in Housing
Awards Book 1977
RIBA Journal
Feb 1978
Architects' Journal
8 Feb 1978
Building Design
17 Nov 1978
A & U
Dec 1978
New Scientist
Dec 1978
RIBA Journal
Jan 1979
Architects' Journal
10 Oct 1979
Building Design
21 Jan 1983

Chichester Theological College
The Builder (Building)
24 Aug 1962
Interbuild
Jul 1963
Architectural Design
Jul 1963
L'Architecture d'Aujourd'hui
Jul 1965
Architectural Review
Aug 1965
Architect and Building News
11 Aug 1965
Architects' Journal
18 Aug 1965
La Maison
Nov 1965
Progressive Architecture
Apr 1966
Deutsche Bauzeitung
Nov 1966
Art d'Eglise 1967
Baumeister
Apr 1967
Kentiku Architecture
Jan 1968
La Maison
Apr 1968
Zodiac
18 Nov 1968
The Japan Architect
Jan 1970
The Politics of Architecture
by Anthony Jackson,
Architectural Press 1970
Country Life by Michael
Webb 1970
Official Architecture and
Planning
Sep 1971
Student Housing:
Architectural and Social
Aspects by William Mullins
and Phyllis Allen 1971
A Visual History of 20th
Century Architecture by D.
Sharp, Heinemann 1972
Entwurf und Planung:
Studentenheime, Callwey
1973
Tilli Tekniikkaa
Arkkitehtuuria
Jan 1975
25 Years of British
Architecture, RIBA 1977
RIBA Journal
Nov 1980
Architects' Journal
19 Nov 1980

Compton Verney
Financial Times
10 Jul 1989
Daily Telegraph
1 Sep 1989
Country Life
7 Sep 1989
Building Design
15 Sep 1989
The Times
15 Sep 1989
Observer
17 Sep 1989

Sunday Times
7 Sep 1989
Architects' Journal
20 Sep 1989

Cummins Engines
Baumeister
Apr 1978
RIBA Journal
Jun 1978
Building
10 Nov 1978
RIBA Journal
Jan 1979
Bauen & Wohnen
Apr 1979
Building with Steel
Jul 1979
Architects' Journal
2 Apr 1980
Building Design
14 Nov 1980
Building
21 Nov 1980
Building with Steel
2 Nov 1980
Acciaio
Feb 1980
Parametro
May 1980
The Structural Engineer
Oct 1981
Architectural Review
Feb 1982
Architectural Journal
17 Feb 1982
Building
19 Feb 1982
Design
Feb 1982
Building Design
5 Feb 1982
Observer Colour Supplement
2 May 1982
L'Architecture d'Aujourd'hui
Jun 1982
A & U
Jul 1982
Techniques & Architecture
Jun 1982
Architects' Journal
16 Jun 1984
SD Space Design
Jan 1985
Lieux de Travail 1986
Engineering and Architecture
1987

Docklands Light Railway
Building Design
6 Jan 1989
Design Week
6 Jan 1989
Building Design
4 Aug 1989
Architecture Today
Apr 1990

Dover Heritage Centre
Building Design
24 Mar 1989
The Times
13 Mar 1989
Dover Express
30 Dec 1988

Observer
20 Aug 1989
Architects' Journal
Jun 1989
The Times
3 Jun 1989
The Times
20 Jun 1989
Building
19 Jan 1990

Dunstan Road Houses
Architectural Review
Jan 1966
Architectural Review
Sep 1970
Concrete Quarterly
Oct/Dec 1971
Financial Times
23 Jan 1972
L'Architecture d'Aujourd'hui
Dec 1971/Jan 1972
House Builder
May 1973
Entwurf und Planung
Mehrfamilienhäuser: Häuser
in Reihen Kettenhäuser
Häusergruppen, Callwey 1973
The Buildings of England:
Oxfordshire by Jennifer
Sherwood and Nikolaus
Pevsner 1974
Baumeister
Aug 1979

Eastfield County Primary School
Kentiku Architecture
Jan 1968
Architects' Journal
29 Oct 1969
L'Architecture d'Aujourd'hui
Feb/Mar 1971

Embassy, Moscow
Building Design
10 Jun 1988
The Times
22 Jun 1988
Ham and High
13 Jan 1989

Exhibitions
Architectural Review
Oct 1961
The Artist
Oct 1961

Felmore Housing
RIBA Journal 1978
RIBA Journal 1979
Architects' Journal
10 Oct 1979
Building Magazine
19 Oct 1979
Building Design
4 Jul 1980
A & U
Dec 1978
Building Services &
Environmental Engineering
Nov 1980
L'Industria delle Contruzione
Nov 1980

A & U
Oct 1981
The Economist
6 Mar 1982
Architektur & Wettbewerbe
Dec 1982

Habitat Warehouse, Showroom, Offices
Financial Times
30 Jul 1974
Building
16 Aug 1974
Architectural Review
Aug 1974
Design
Aug 1974
Domus
Sep 1974
International Asbestos-
Cement Review
Jul 1975
Building
19 Mar 1976
Baumeister
Oct 1976
Architectural Journal
Nov 1976
Building Week
12 Nov 1976
Space Design
Aug 1978
Building Design
12 Nov 1976
Financial Times
11 Nov 1976
Architects' Journal
2 Apr 1980
RIBA Journal
Jun 1981
Building Design
11 Dec 1981

Hooke Park College
Private Eye
4 Nov 1983
Building Design
18 Nov 1983
Building
18 Nov 1983
Architects' Journal
21 & 28 Nov 1983
Architects' Journal
21 & 28 Dec 1983
Building Design
10 Feb 1984
Design Magazine
Jul 1984
Designing
Summer 1984
Chartered Surveyor Weekly
4 Oct 1984
Crafts
Jan/Feb 1985
Building
4 Oct 1985
The Times
16 Aug 1985
Building Design
18 Oct 1985
Sunday Times
1 Dec 1985
New Scientist
12 Dec 1985

Observer
15 Dec 1985
Architectural Review
Jan 1986
Woodland Management
22 Feb 1986
Sunday Times
13 Jul 1986
Woodworker
Mar 1986
Woodworker
Apr 1986
Vogue
Jul 1986
Building Design
Jun 1987
Construction News Products
Sep 1986
Architects' Journal
5 Nov 1986
Architects' Journal
3 Dec 1986
Detail
Nov/Dec 1987
Interiors Quarterly 1987 No. 9
Progressive Architecture
Jan 1988
SD
Jan 1989
Design Week
Mar 1989
Country Times
Apr 1989
Architects' Journal Focus
May 1989
Detail Tragwerke 1989
Building Design Supplement
Jun 1990
Deutsche Bauzeitung
Jul 1990
Architectural Review
Sep 1990

House in Wicklow
Architectural Review
Jan 1980
Building Design
16 Oct 1981

John Lewis Kingston
Surrey Comet
1 Dec 1979
Architects' Journal
12 Dec 1979
Building Design
11 Jan 1980
RIBA Journal
Feb 1981
L'Architecture d'Aujourd'hui
Dec 1984
Chartered Surveyor
18 Apr 1985
Architects' Journal
30 Apr 1986
Building Design
25 Apr 1986
Construction News
4 Jun 1987
RIBA Retail Supplement 1987
Sunday Times
15 Jan 1989
Financial Times
30 Mar 1989
Concrete Quarterly
Winter 1989

Architects' Journal
26 Sep 1990
Building
14 Sep 1990
Building Design Supplement
Sep 1990

J. Sainsbury Supermarket
Architects' Journal
13 Oct 1982
Architectural Review
May 1983
Architects' Journal
20 Jun 1984
Building Design
2 Nov 1984
Architects' Journal
5 Dec 1984
Tubular Structures BSC
Aug 1985
The Times
25 Sep 1985
L'Industria delle Construzioni
Oct 1985
Ham and High
3 Jan 1986
BCSA News
Feb 1986
Architecture Contemporaine
1985/1986
Building Design
5 Dec 1986
Architects' Journal
10 Dec 1986
BADA 1986
The Independent
24 Mar 1988
Detail Tragwerke 1989

Kasmin Gallery
Architectural Review
Nov 1963
Light and Lighting
Mar 1967
Kentiku Architecture
Jan 1968

Keble College
Architectural Review
Jul 1973
Baumeister
Oct 1973
Architecture and Urbanism
Feb 1974
The Buildings of England:
Oxfordshire by Jennifer
Sherwood and Nikolaus
Pevsner 1974
Daily Telegraph Magazine
Mar 1974
L'Architecture d'Aujourd'hui
Sep 1974
Tilli
Jan 1975
Building Design
May 1977
Architectural Review
Dec 1977
25 Years of British
Architecture, RIBA 1977
New Architecture in Oxford
by Philip Opher and David
Reed, Oxford Poly 1977
Baumeister
May 1978

Sunday Times Magazine
13 Aug 1978
Guardian
14 Aug 1978
L'Industria della Costruzioni
Jan 1979

Maidenhead Library
Tubular Structures
18 Apr 1971
Architectural Review
May 1974
Architecture Plus
Sep/Oct 1974
Brick Bulletin
Sep 1974
Tilli
Mar 1975
Baumeister
May 1975
Glasforum
Nov 1975
Deutsche Bauzeitschrift
Jul 1976
Baumeister
Jul 1978
L'Industria delle Construzioni
Jul/Aug 1979
Architecture and the Human
Dimension by Peter F. Smith,
G. Godwin Ltd. 1979

Mary Rose Ship Museum
Building Design
21 Mar 1980
Architectural Review
Jan 1982
Building Design
19 Nov 1982
Illustrated London News
Oct 1982

National Gallery Extension
Architects' Journal
25 Aug 1982
Building Design
27 Aug 1982
Financial Times
31 Aug 1982
Architects' Journal
1 Sep 1982
Building Design
3 Sep 1982
Building Design
10 Sep 1982
Architects' Journal
15 Sep 1982
Financial Times
3 Oct 1982
Architects' Journal
27 Oct 1982
Progressive Architecture
Oct 1982
Building
27 Aug 1982
Building
22 Oct 1982
City Limits
19 Nov 1982
Illustrated London News
Oct 1982
Architectural Review
Dec 1982

Glass Age
Dec 1982
Architects' Journal
22 & 29 Dec 1982
New Society
5 Jan 1983
Architects' Journal
5 Jan 1983
Building Design
7 Jan 1983
Financial Times
10 Jan 1983
Building Design
14 Jan 1983
Building Design
28 Jan 1983
Glass Age
Feb 1983
Architects' Journal
27 Jul 1983
Blueprint
Oct 1983
Building Design
9 Dec 1983
Architects' Journal
14 Dec 1983
Building Design
16 Dec 1983
Architektur & Wettbewerbe
Dec 1983
Illustrated London News
Jan 1984
RIBA Journal
Jan 1984
Blueprint
Feb 1984
Architectural Review
Feb 1984
Architects' Journal
22 Feb 1984
Baumeister
Mar 1984
Architects' Journal
11 Apr 1984
Architects' Journal
18 Apr 1984
Architects' Journal
25 Apr 1984
RIBA Journal
Apr 1984
Architects' Journal
6 Jun 1984
RIBA Journal
Jun 1984
Architects' Journal
26 Sep 1984
RIBA Journal
Jul 1984
Building Design
4 Oct 1984
Building Design
12 Oct 1984
Architects' Journal
19 & 26 Dec 1984
Building Design
14 Dec 1984
Architects' Journal
2 & 9 Jan 1985
Art & Design
Feb 1985
Architects' Journal
10 & 17 Apr 1985

Blueprint
Apr 1985
London Standard
21 Oct 1985
Architects' Journal
27 May 1987
Archithese
Nov/Dec 1987
Blueprint
Sep 1987
Building Design
4 Nov 1988
Sunday Times
30 Oct 1988
The New York Review
19 Jan 1989
Building Design
9 Jun 1989
Building Design Supplement
Feb 1990

National Garden Festival Festival Hall, Stoke on Trent
Building Design
30 Nov 1984
Evening Standard
7 Dec 1984
Building Design
24 May 1985
Architects' Journal
6 Nov 1985
Financial Times
16 Nov 1985
Architects' Journal
20 Nov 1985
Guardian
26 Nov 1985
Building Design
6 Dec 1985
Building
14 Feb 1986
Ham and High
9 May 1986
Art and Design
May 1986
Technology in Architecture
1986
Building Design
19 Sep 1986
RIBA Directory 1986

Nebenzahl House
Architectural Review
Aug 1975
Baumeister
Dec 1976
A & U
Sep 1977
RIBA 25 Years of British
Architecture 1977
L'Architecture d'Aujourd'hui
Apr 1978
Space Design
Aug 1978
L'Industria delle Construzione
Nov 1978
Baumeister
Dec 1978

North Pole Depot British Rail
Building Design
8 Dec 1989

The Independent
13 Dec 1989
Building Design
16 Feb 1990
Sunday Times
18 Feb 1990

Portsmouth Polytechnic
L'Architecture d'Aujourd'hui
Sep/Oct 1974
Architects' Journal
26 Jul 1978
Building Design
4 Aug 1978
What's New In Building
Oct 1978
Architectural Review
Apr 1979
Contemporary Architecture
1979
Architects' Journal
4 Apr 1979
Baumeister
Dec 1979
Detail
May/Jun 1980
A & U
Oct 1979

Post Office Headquarters
Architectural Review
Jul 1975
Architects' Journal
10 Sep 1975
Building Design
27 Oct 1978
The Architect
Apr 1975
Space Design
Aug 1978

Redcar Library
Architectural Review
Jul 1971
The Architectural Forum
Nov 1971
L'Architecture d'Aujourd'hui
Dec 1971/Jan 1972
Baumeister
Jan 1974

**Roman Catholic
Chaplaincy**
L'Architecture d'Aujourd'hui
Jul 1965
Architekten
19 Sep 1966
Building
2 Dec 1966
Kentiku Architecture
Jan 1968
Student Housing:
Architectural and Social
Aspects by William Mullins
and Phyllis Allen 1971
L'Architecture d'Aujourd'hui
Dec 1971/Jan 1972
Architectural Review
Dec 1972
Entwurf und Planung:
Studentenheime, Callwey
1973

The Buildings of England:
Oxfordshire by Jennifer
Sherwood and Nikolaus
Pevsner 1974
New Architecture in Oxford
by David Reed and Philip
Opher, Oxford Poly 1977

St. Andrew's College
Architectural Review
Jun 1976
Baumeister
Feb 1977
SD
Aug 1978
A & U
Jul 1979
Architecture Plus
Sep/Oct 1974
L'Architecture d'Aujourd'hui
Sep/Oct 1974

St. Anne's Church
Progressive Architecture
Jan 1966
Architectural Review
Jan 1966
Architekten
19 Sep 1966
Mosaic
Oct 1966
Kentiku Architecture
Jan 1968
L'Architecture d'Aujourd'hui
Dec 1971/Jan 1972

St. Martin's Youth Project
Architectural Review
Mar 1975

St. Mary's Hospital I.O.W.
Architects' Journal
27 Oct 1982
Link
Oct 1983
British Medical Journal
1 Dec 1984
Crafts
Mar/Apr 1985
Building Design
3 May 1985
Building Design Energy and
Insulation Supplement
May 1985
Building Design
17 May 1985
Interior Design
Mar 1986
IDI 1986
Architects' Journal
7 May 1986
The Best of Health
Feb 1986
Interior Design
Jul/Aug 1987
Arts
18 Jul 1986
British Medical Journal
7 Nov 1987
Islander
Oct/Nov 1987
Hospital Development
Oct 1987
The Independent
6 Oct 1987

Architects' Journal
3 Aug 1988
Good Housekeeping
Jul 1988
Construction News
Sep 1988
Sunday Times
9 Oct 1988
Hospital Development
Mar 1989
Sunday Times
15 Oct 1989
Southern Evening Echo
31 Oct 1989
Southern Evening Echo
10 Nov 1989
Guardian
15 Nov 1989
Architects' Journal
22 Nov 1989
Island Business
Feb/Mar 1990
Link
Apr 1990
Architecture Today
Jun 1990
Hospital Development
Jun 1990
British Medical Journal
14 Jul 1990
The Times
3 Aug 1990
Sunday Times
5 Aug 1990

Stag Place Competition
Daily Telegraph
16 Dec 1985
Building Design
19 Dec 1986
The Architect
Sep 1987
Architectural Review
Jan 1988

Templeton College
Kentiku Architecture
Jan 1968
Architectural Review
Aug 1969
Design
Aug 1969
Architects' Journal
10 Sep 1969
Forum
May 1970
Zinc
Nov 1970
Detail Serie 1970
Merk
May 1971
L'Architecture d'Aujourd'hui
Dec 1971/Jan 1972
Entwurf und Planung:
Studentenheime, Callwey
1973
The Buildings of England:
Oxfordshire by Jennifer
Sherwood and Nikolaus
Pevsner 1974
New Architecture in Oxford
by David Reed and Philip
Opher, Oxford Poly 1977

**Trinity College Arts
Faculty Building**
Building Design
13 Aug 1971
Building and Contract Journal
19 Aug 1971
Building
25 Feb 1972
Building
24 Mar 1978
Architecture in Ireland
Jun 1978
Plan
Aug 1978
Building Design
Jun 1978
Trade and Industry
25 Aug 1978
Architects' Journal
15 Nov 1978
RIBA Journal
Jan 1979
Build (Irish)
Jul 1978
Irish H & V News
Oct 1978
Architectural Review
Jul 1979
Architects' Journal
18 Jul 1979
Architects' Journal
19 Sep 1979
A & U
Oct 1979
Baumeister
Dec 1979
Architecture Contemporaine
1980/81
Architektur & Wettbewerbe
1980
Detail 1981
L'Industria italiana del
Cemento
Oct 1988

**Trinity College Berkeley
Library**
Architect and Building News
14 Jan 1961
Architects' Journal
15 Jun 1961
The Builder (Building)
16 Jun 1961
L'Architecture d'Aujourd'hui
Jul 1965
Guardian
24 May 1965
Architect and Building News
Aug 1966
RIBA Journal
Sep 1966
Architectural Review
Oct 1967
The Architectural Forum
Oct 1967
Architectural Design
Oct 1967
Architect and Building News
11 Oct 1967
Architects' Journal
11 Oct 1967
Architects' Journal
18 Oct 1967
Building
20 Oct 1967

Concrete Quarterly
Oct/Dec 1967
L'Architecture d'Aujourd'hui
Apr/May 1968
Progressive Architecture
Oct 1967
Sunday Times Supplement
4 Feb 1968
Kentiku Architecture
Jan 1968
Bauwelt
May 1968
Architect and Building News
Sep 1968
Moebel Interior Design
Nov 1968
Zodiac
18 Nov 1968
Architecture Actualités
Jan/Feb 1969
The Architectural Forum
Dec 1969
The Japan Architect
Jan 1970
L'Industria Italiana del
Cemento
Apr 1971
Building
25 Feb 1972
Architects' Journal
26 Jul 1972
Penguin Dictionary of
Architecture Pevsner, Honour,
Fleming 2nd Ed. 1972
Architects' Journal
19 Nov 1980
Irish Architect
Jun/Jul 1988

Whitmore Court Housing
Kentiku Architecture
Jan 1968
Recent East Anglian
Buildings 1977
A & U
Sep 1977

W. H. Smith Offices
Architects' Journal
7 Sep 1983
Architectural Review Preview
Jan 1984
Designer's Journal
May 1986
RIBA Journal
Mar 1988
The Times
23 Oct 1987
Techniques & Architecture
Aug/Sep 1988

Biographies

Peter Ahrends RIBA AA Dip(Hons) Architectural Association School of Architecture 1956; born April 1933; Founding Partner of Ahrends Burton & Koralek 1961; part-time teaching at AA School of Architecture 1960-69; Member of Council of the Architectural Association 1962-74; Master Class, School of Architecture, Canterbury School of Art 1978-81; Master Class Workshop, Department of Architecture, Plymouth Polytechnic 1982-88; Bartlett Professor of Architecture, Bartlett School of Architecture & Planning, University College London 1986-89; currently Member Design Council

Richard Burton RIBA AA Dip(Hons) FRSA Architectural Association School of Architecture 1956; born November 1933; Founding Partner of Ahrends Burton & Koralek 1961; co-ordinator of RIBA Energy Initiative, Member Science Research Council Building Committee, Member Watt Committee on Energy 1976-79; RIBA Presidential Adviser on Energy Matters 1980-81; Leader CUDAT, Southampton 1985; Member RUDAT for Steel Valley, Pittsburg, USA 1988; currently Chairman Arts Council National 'Percent for Art' Steering Group, Governor Building Centre Trust, Founder Director Building Use Studies Limited, Member Royal Jubilee Trust – Faith in the City Housing Estates Steering Committee

Paul Koralek CBE ARA RIBA AA Dip(Hons) Architectural Association School of Architecture 1956; born April 1933; Marcel Breuer, New York 1959-60; Founding Partner of Ahrends Burton & Koralek 1961; Member RIBA London Environment Group 1969-71; Member British Rail Environment Panel 1985-88; elected Associate of the Royal Academy 1986; currently Assessor for Civic Trust Awards, Trustee Building Industry Youth Trust, Member Cardiff Bay Development Corporation Design and Architectural Review Panel, Member ARCUK Board of Architectural Education

Paul Drake RIBA AA Dip Architectural Association School of Architecture 1959; born April 1934; joined Ahrends Burton & Koralek 1962; Associate Ahrends Burton & Koralek 1967; Partner Ahrends Burton & Koralek 1974; part-time teaching at Architectural Association 1965, Kingston Polytechnic 1980 and Thames Polytechnic 1985

John Hermsen FRIBA ACI Arb Royal West of England Academy School of Architecture 1956; born August 1933; elected FRIBA 1969; group leader National Building Agency 1964-71; member BSI Committee 3921 1969-71; joined Ahrends Burton & Koralek 1971; partner Ahrends Burton and Koralek 1974; associate Chartered Institute of Arbitrators 1984

Patrick Stubbings RIBA DipArch Hammersmith College of Art & Building 1957; born April 1935; National Building Agency 1962-66; joined Ahrends Burton & Koralek 1966; Associate Ahrends Burton & Koralek 1969; Partner Ahrends Burton & Koralek 1974

David Cruse RIBA DipArch Polytechnic of Central London School of Architecture 1977; born December 1951; joined Ahrends Burton & Koralek 1978; part-time teaching at Polytechnic of Central London 1979-82 and at Cambridge School of Architecture 1987; Associate Ahrends Burton & Koralek 1986

Christine Price RIBA DipArch Birmingham School of Architecture 1964; joined Ahrends Burton & Koralek 1975; Associate Ahrends Burton & Koralek 1986

Jeremy Peacock RIBA AA Dip Architectural Association School of Architecture 1978; born January 1954; Associate Ahrends Burton & Koralek 1987; '40 under 40' RIBA Exhibition 1985; part-time teaching at Bartlett School of Architecture & Planning 1988-89

David Adams
Nadia Alami
Allessandra Alborghetti
Nazar Alikhan
James Allman
Graham Anthony
Bruce Ash
John Attwood
Robert Axten
Mark Bagguley
Isabella Baron
Peggy Bateman
Hilary Bateson
Louise Beaton
Peter Behrman
Andrew Bell
Christine Bellamy
Martin Benson
Colin Bex
Sarah Beynon
David Bishop
Margaret Bisset
Katie Blach
Jeannette Black
Margaret Blanch
Debbie Borst
Christopher Boulton
Manuel Bouza
Matthew Bowers
Michael Bradley
Lester Alan Brauer
Stephen Brigley
Derek Briscoe
Tress Brokenshire
Massimo Brooks
Michael Brown
Walter Buck
Diana Burdett-Coutts
Timothy Bushe
Lucian Butterlin
Carl Callaghan
Francesca Camilleri-Preziosi
David Castle
Hilary Castle
Lorraine Caunter
Nat Chard
Neil Charles-Jones
Afzal Chaudhry
Catherine Clarke
Johnnie Clarke
Janet Cockerill
Lynn Cohen
Clifford Cole
Chris Cole
Rob Cole
Rosie Collings
Tina Colquhoun
Eamonn Connolly
Nick Cooney
Stuart Cooper
Nancy Copplestone
Athol Corbett
Jon Corpe
Alan Cox
Cathy Cox
Nigel Cox

Sue Cracknell
Janet Crickmay
Anne Crosbie
Colin Cunningham
Mark Cuthbert
Dan Darin-Drabkin
Hugh Davies
Robert Davys
Wolfgang Deering
Gregory des Jardins
John Dewe-Mathews
Michael Dillon
Olive Drake
Reuvens Druckmann
Sally Dryland
Mark Dziewulski
Florian Eames
Colin Eastwick
Richard Eastwick
Harriet Edgerley
Ian Edmundson
Kate Edwards
Gad Einbinder
Janet Elliott
Peter Ellis
Carlos Elsesser
Janet Evans
Michael Fiertag
Roy Fleetwood
Frances Fogarty
Roger Foster
Simon Foxell
Graham Francis
Michelle Francis
Anthony Ffrench-Constant
Camilo Gallardo
Frazer Gardiner
Jackie Gately
Clare Gerrard
Scott Gill
Darius Gilmont
Christine Goodliff
Michael Goold
Clive Gray
Jack Greenaway
Walter Greenhill
Jane Greening
Mary Griffin
Mandy Griffith
Bruce Haden
Rolfe Haefeli
Ben Hamilton
Andrew Harding
Adam Hardy
John Harris
Matthew Harris
Antonio Harrison
Valerie Harrison
William Harrison
Darrell Hawthorne
Michael Healy
Filip Henley
Leila Herman
Henry Hertzberg
Polly Hewitt
Roger Hibberd

Eric Hill
Keith Hodson
John Howard
Steve Howarth
Jane Howson
Edwin Hughes
Francesca Hughes
Kirsten Hughes
William Hughes
Maria Hugo
Graham Hussey
Amanda Hutton
Ewart Hutton
James Hutton
Steven Jacobs
Dominic Jackson
Edward Jakmauh
Stephen Jamieson
David Jenkins
David Jennings
Clare Jones
Michael Jones
Trevor Jones
George Kasabov
Kasmai
Raj Kaushik
Mark Kelly
Douglas Keys
Angela Kidner
Tony Kiley
Kimura
Johannes Knesl
Tom Knott
Anna Koutelieri
Lucy Koralek
Bob Kovanic
Ljiljana Kudic
Elizabeth Lake
Harvey Langston Jones
Dean La Tourelle
Cora Laven
Mark Lecchini
Sally Ledger-Lomas
Thomas Lee
Jill Leslie
Anthony Leslie
David Leuthold
Julian Lipscombe
Christina Little
Michael Livingstone
Heidi Locher
Ernst Lohse
Deborah Loudan
Pauline Love
Luke Lowings
Colin Lumley
Duncan Macaulay
Michael Macauley
Marnie Macdonald
Catherine MacDougall
Kate Macintosh
Anna Maclean
Rainer Magiera
Libby Maher
Tina Marden-King
Karen Marler

Elizabeth Marley
Jim Marriot
Huren Marsh
John Martineau
Penelope Martin-Jones
Eamonn McCann
Terry McCarthy
Kate McCormack
Mike McCormack
Malcolm McGowan
Nigel McKenzie
Leslie Meldrum
Chris Miers
Andy Mindel
Blake Minton
Hannah Minton
Linda Moore
William Moorwood
Clive Morgan
Hugh Morgan
Michael Morris
Phillip Motyer
Pearse Murray
Len Newsome
Stephen Nicoll
Jim O'Donohoe
Kojo Ofusduhene
Derek Orbach
Brian O'Reilly
Steve Oyekanmi
Jenny Papaioannou
Mungo Park
Andrew Parker
Anna-Louise Parkin
Norman Partridge
Richard Partridge
Richard Patterson
Richard Paxton
Lucy Pedler
Patricia Peters
Dian Phillips
Sue Phillips
Benedicte Pitman
Zofia Pogoda
Nicolas Pople
Teresa Pritchard
Karel Pruner
Caroline Pullen
Sarah Quilley
Caroline Raffan
Antoine Raffoul
Haji Abdul Rahim
John Randle
Paul Rayer
Carmella Rejwan
John Renton
Brian Reynolds
John Ricketts
Dan Roberts
David Roessler
Kirsty Ross
Richard Russell
Mike Russum
John Ryan
Jill Sack
David St. John

Michael Salter
Barbara Sawden
Douglas Schwab
John Shaw
Martin Short
Elizabeth Shuker
Louise Silvester
Emil Simeloff
Martin Simpson
Judi Sissons
David Soffer
Nicky Southin
Sharon Staddon
Martin Starr
Richard Sterry
Nick Stevens
Robert Stevenson
Margaret Stonborough
Timothy Strangward
Mary Stutter
Don Taylor
Leslie Taylor
William Taylor
Dharini Thiru
David Thomas
Ray Thomson
Farhad Toussi
Peter Town
George Tsoutsis
David Tucker
Patrick Turner
Kay Tyler
Lynn Tyzack
Eric Underwood
Martin Ungless
Allen van der Steen
Jill Vickerson
Rudolphe Victorri
Peter Wadley
Hugh Waine
Joan Waite
Donal Walsh
Geoffrey Ward
Jonathen Watson
Gayle Webber
Michael Wells
Victoria Wharton
Thalia Whitaker
Roger Willard
Pat Williams
Neridah Windass
Anstice Winter
Martyn Wood
Elizabeth Woodman
John Worthington
Nicola Worton
Gareth Wright
James Wright
Joe Wright
Richard Wright
Woon Juen Yee
Tom Young
Pat Young
Mei Yu

We have tried to include the names of everyone who has worked at Ahrends Burton and Koralek and regret any omissions.

Credits

All photographs by **John Donat** except:

Bob Bell p.144

Barry Bulley p.118

Martin Charles cover: top centre, pp.78, 80, 89 top, 107, 108 top, 120 bottom 1&r, 121 1&R

Peter Cook cover: middle centre, pp.139, 140, 141, 142 centre, 143, 146

John Ford most of the photographs of drawings

Chris Gascoigne/Arcaid pp.34-35, 120 top, 121 bottom, 122

Terry Grimwood cover: bottom centre, pp.128, 130, 131 all except top 1, 133

Barbara Luthy pp.49 top & bottom, 56 centre

William Moorwood p.146 bottom

Owens of Wishaw cover: top 1

Stephen Parker p.174 centre 1&r, bottom 1

Adrian Peacock p.174 centre & bottom r

Jeremy Peacock pp.130 top r, 150

David Price p.174 bottom centre

Antoine Raffoul pp.38 lower 1, 39, 43 top, 44, 47, 52, 53, 57 bottom, 67 bottom, 71 top & bottom, 82, 87, 90 bottom, 91 bottom, 92 bottom, 94, 95, 98 top 1, 100 top, 101, 105 bottom, 114, 115

Walter Rawlings cover: centre r, pp.36, 41

Martin Weinreb pp.138, 139 bottom

Front Cover left to right

Top

| Cummins Engines | Keble College | National Gallery |

Middle

| Nebenzahl House | J. Sainsbury Canterbury | Berkeley Library Trinity College |

Bottom

| Templeton College | St. Mary's Hospital Isle of Wight | Hooke Park College |

Page 2

J. Sainsbury Canterbury

Page 6

Keble College

Pages 34-35

John Lewis Kingston

Page 173

Burton House

Back Cover left to right

Top

| La Fleuryais Nantes | Royal Victoria Dock Landmark Building | National Gallery |

Middle

| Chalvedon Housing | St. Mary's Hospital Isle of Wight | Burton House |

Bottom

| J. Sainsbury Canterbury | John Lewis Kingston | Berkeley Library Trinity College |

Designer
James Sutton

Our thanks to
Jill Sack *for her editorial contribution to the book.*